Exploring
THE MISSISSIPPI RIVER VALLEY

Rose Blue and Corinne J. Naden

Raintree
Chicago, Illinois

© 2003 Raintree
Published by Raintree,
a division of Reed Elsevier, Inc.
Chicago, Illinois
Customer Service 888-454-2279
Visit our website at www.raintreelibrary.com

For information, address the publisher:
Raintree
100 N. LaSalle, Suite 1200
Chicago IL 60602

Printed and bound in the United States.

07 06 05 04 03
10 9 8 7 6 5 4 3 2 1

Library of Congress Cataloging-in-Publication Data:
Blue, Rose.
   Exploring the Mississippi River Valley / Rose Blue
and Corinne J. Naden.
      v. cm. -- (Exploring the Americas)
Includes bibliographical references (p.   ) and index.
Contents: Prologue: who found it? -- Jacques
Marquette and Louis Jolliet: where the river flows
(1541) -- Rene-Robert Cavelier, Sieur de la Salle:
France enters its claim (1682) -- Pierre le Moyne
d'Iberville: where the river ends (1697) -- Jean-
Baptiste le Moyne de Bienville: the road to New
Orleans (1699) -- Henry Rowe Schoolcraft: where the
river begins (1832) -- Epilogue: what did they find? --
Important events in the exploration of the Mississippi
River Valley -- Important sites along the Mississippi
River system.
   ISBN 0-7398-4949-2 (HC), 1-4109-0043-6 (Pbk.)
   1. Mississippi River Valley--Discovery and
exploration--Juvenile literature. 2. Explorers--
Mississippi River Valley--Biography--Juvenile
literature. [1. Mississippi River Valley--Discovery and
exploration. 2. Explorers.] I. Naden, Corinne J. II.
Title.
F351 .B58 2003
977'.01--dc21
                              2002013352

Acknowledgments
The author and publishers are grateful to the
following for permission to reproduce copyright
material:

Cover photographs by Hulton Archive/Getty Images

pp. 4, 51 Nathan Benn/Corbis; pp. 5, 9, 19, 33, 46,
52, 54 Corbis; pp. 6, 14, 34, 42, 45 Hulton
Archive/Getty Images; p. 11 Dave G. Houser/Corbis;
p. 12 State Historical Society of Iowa; p. 17 Layne
Kennedy/Corbis; p. 18 Hulton-Deutsch
Collection/Corbis; pp. 21, 28, 38 Bettmann/Corbis;
pp. 23, 40 The Granger Collection, NY; pp. 24, 36
North Wind Picture Archives; p. 26 Raymond
Gehman/Corbis; p. 31 Eranian Philippe/Corbis
SYGMA; p. 39 James P. Rowan; p. 44 D. Donne
Bryant/DDB Stock; p. 47 SuperStock; p. 56 David
Muench/Corbis

Photo research by Alyx Kellington

Some words are shown in bold, like **this.** You can
find out what they mean by looking in the Glossary.

Contents

Prologue: Who Found It? 4

JACQUES MARQUETTE and LOUIS JOLLIET:
Where the River Flows (1672–1673) 8

RENE-ROBERT CAVELIER, SIEUR DE LA SALLE:
France Enters Its Claim (1679–1687) 19

PIERRE LE MOYNE D'IBERVILLE:
Where the River Ends (1686–1707) 34

JEAN-BAPTISTE LE MOYNE DE BIENVILLE:
The Road to New Orleans (1696–1743) 42

HENRY ROWE SCHOOLCRAFT:
Where the River Begins (1817–1832) 52

Epilogue: What Did They Find? 58

Important Events in the Exploration
of the Mississippi River Valley .59

Important Sites Along the Mississippi River System 60

Mississippi River System Fact List 61

Glossary 62

Further Reading 63

Index 64

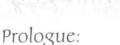

Prologue:
Who Found It?

Who found it? And what had they found? When early explorers from Europe first saw the coast of North America, most of them thought it was Asia. They were overjoyed. A northern route to the Far East would save time and money for anyone trading there. It would also mean a lot of money for the explorer. But, of course, the early explorers had not reached Asia. Their joy turned to frustration time and again. It took a while before they realized that instead of Asia, they had sailed into what was for them a new world. Some began to look for ways to

get through that new world to the East. Others began to look at the new world itself. When they did, they had no idea how big it would turn out to be.

This is the story of how six explorers began to find out about the size of the North American continent. It was quite a surprise. Except for the mighty Atlantic Ocean—and they did not even know how large that was—the world for most of the early explorers appeared small in comparison. For instance, Jean Bienville, who founded the city of New Orleans, came from France. He could not have known it at the time, of course,

Almost one-third of the United States' freshwater flows through the confluence of the Mississippi and Ohio rivers, near Cairo, Illinois.

but his entire country is smaller than the state of Texas. When Jacques Marquette and Louis Jolliet began their travels down the Mississippi River, they would have been surprised to discover that it flowed on for 2,350 miles (3,782 kilometers). With its main tributaries, the Missouri and the Ohio Rivers, the entire river system is over 5,550 miles (8,932 kilometers) long. It is North America's major river system and one of the world's largest. But for the explorers, size was not the only surprise of the newly found continent. They ran into a number of remarkable discoveries in and around the Mississippi River Valley.

These six explorers were not the first of the early Europeans to see the Mississippi. The Spanish conquistador Hernando de Soto first saw it in 1541. But he is known mainly for his explorations of the southeastern United States and of Central America and Peru. Nor were these six the only early Europeans to see the mighty river. Many explorers had at least a small part in charting its course. But Marquette, Jolliet, La Salle, Iberville, and Bienville played major roles in the exploration and future settlement of the Mississippi River Valley. Schoolcraft is included because, even though his role was small, he did find where the great river began.

First on any list of Mississippi River explorers are the names of Marquette

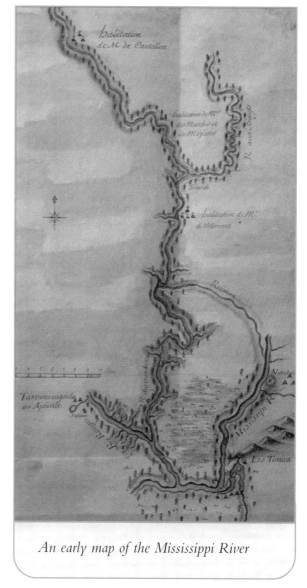

An early map of the Mississippi River

and Jolliet, one from France and one from Canada. They mapped the course of the river that cuts north to south through the center of the United States—the mighty Mississippi. Their story begins in the 1670s. At the time, much of what would become the United

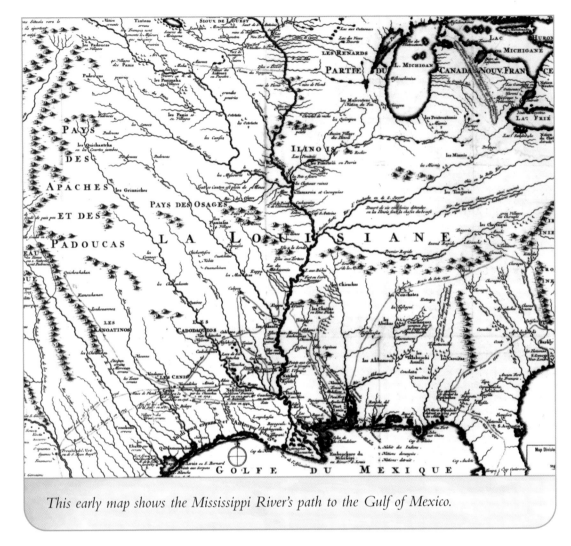

This early map shows the Mississippi River's path to the Gulf of Mexico.

States was still an uncharted wilderness. A little later, Frenchman Robert La Salle explored and claimed a huge parcel of land in America. He took it for his king and named it Louisiana. Then came Pierre Iberville, who was more soldier than explorer. He explored as far north as Hudson Bay in Canada and as far south as the **delta** of the Mississippi River. He founded the first permanent French settlement in Louisiana. It was not far from the site of present-day New Orleans. Many years later, Bienville, Iberville's youngest brother, founded New Orleans and even made it the capital of the colony for a time.

These stories of exploring the Mississippi River Valley end with Henry Schoolcraft and his search for its source in 1832. More than 150 years had passed since Marquette and Jolliet. Much had changed. By Schoolcraft's time, the United States of America was an independent nation with 24 states, and Andrew Jackson was president.

Who were these six men—Marquette and Jolliet, La Salle, Iberville, Bienville, and Schoolcraft? They were all different, from different backgrounds. Marquette was a French priest and missionary. Jolliet renounced the priesthood for a life in the wilderness. Iberville, a naval commander, and Bienville were sons of a French colonial leader. Schoolcraft was an ethnologist from New York; he studied races of people and wrote a good deal about the native peoples of the North American plains. But for all their differences, these men had much in common. They were adventurers, ready to take dangerous journeys, willing to find out "what was on the other side." Remember, too, that they explored under fairly primitive conditions. Most of those who traveled the Mississippi valley in the early days did so in canoes or on horseback. None of them had maps of this unexplored territory. There were no modern means of communication. They faced danger at nearly every bend of the river or over the next hill. Yet, for whatever reason, these adventurers had a need to find out about the unknown. That is what an explorer does.

Most of the time, exploration is a step-by-step process, each adventurer learning a little from the one before. Since 1492 when Christopher Columbus sailed across the Atlantic Ocean, people began talking about a "new" land between Europe and Asia—even if they did not know what it was. Ferdinand Magellan sailed away from Spain in 1519. He died on the voyage, but his ship returned to Spain in 1521. It had sailed around the world. Each new discovery led to another adventure, and the same process continues today. The United States put a man on the moon in 1969. But Neil Armstrong could never have gotten there without all the failed rocket tests and all the successful manned flights before him. That is how exploration works.

Although we often say that explorers "discovered" a place, we know that in most cases they were not the first to get there. Native Americans, for instance, lived in North America long before the early European explorers arrived. But the explorers did something that had not been done before. They mapped and examined what they had found. They wrote in their journals. They brought back stories that told of strange and unbelievable sights. In so doing, they opened up new territory for all those hardy, brave, sometimes cruel, and often reckless adventurers who would come after them. The world would never be the same again. That is why the explorers are so important. They changed everything.

Chapter One
Jacques Marquette and Louis Jolliet
Where the River Flows (1672–1673)

It has many names: Great River, Father of the Waters, Ole Man River. People write songs about it. Mark Twain wrote a book about living on it. Some people swim in it; some fish in it; others take paddlewheel boat cruises on it. Industries are built along its banks and so are houses. It has been photographed millions of times from thousands of different angles. People praise it for the rich farmland along its shores and curse it for the terrible floods that carry away that same rich soil, along with people and property. It is the Mississippi, America's major river system.

Running down the center of the United States, the river system has three main branches: the Missouri, the Mississippi, and the Ohio. From southwestern Montana, the Missouri River flows 2,315 miles (3,726 kilometers) to meet the Mississippi at St. Louis, Missouri. The Mississippi has been on a 1,215-mile (1,955-kilometer) journey of its own from northwestern Minnesota. About 200 miles (322 kilometers) south of St. Louis, the Ohio joins the other two after traveling about 981 miles (1,579 kilometers) from Pittsburgh, Pennsylvania. The name of the main river comes from the Ojibway Indians of Wisconsin, who called it *Missi Sipi*, meaning great river or big water.

The Ojibway knew about the Mississippi as did other native peoples. When European explorers and early white settlers came to North America, they heard tales about a great south-flowing body of water. But where was it? Did it flow to the Gulf of Mexico? To the Pacific Ocean? Where did it begin and end? In May 1673, Jacques Marquette and Louis Jolliet went in search of the answers. They became the first explorers to record accurate data on the course of the Mississippi River.

The missionary priest

Jacques Marquette (1637–1675) was a Jesuit priest, a missionary. He was born in Laon, France, the youngest child of Nicolas and Rose de la Salle Marquette. His ancestors had lived in that region since the 1300s. Jacques was a thoughtful and gentle young man who told his family at age seventeen that he wanted to enter the priesthood. This was quite surprising to the Marquettes. They had always been government officials and warriors. However, his mother's family was religiously inclined. So, Jacques was sent to the city of Nancy to study. In 1656, he was ordained and went to Pont Mousson where he studied philosophy and then took on teaching duties in Rheims and other cities.

Even more than he wanted to be a priest, Marquette longed to be a missionary. He said he wanted to die in the wilderness like the great Roman Catholic missionary Saint Francis Xavier (1506–1552). If Marquette was looking for a place to die in the wilderness like Xavier, what Europeans were calling the New World seemed a good choice. He volunteered for missionary duty among the Native American tribes and got his wish in 1666. His superiors selected him for service in New France.

New France was the name given to the first French colonies on the continent of North America. Initially just along the St. Lawrence River and in Newfoundland and Acadia (Nova Scotia and later New Brunswick), they expanded to include much of the Great Lakes region. Jacques Cartier entered the Gulf of St. Lawrence in 1534 and took possession of the area in the name of King Francis I. By the time Marquette arrived, New France had become a royal province by order of King Louis XIV. Probably about 3,000 settlers lived there.

Teaching in the wilderness

After sailing with the royal fleet, Marquette landed in the city of Quebec on September 20, 1666. Canada's oldest city, Quebec was founded on the site of the Indian town of Stadacona and was

Portrait of Jacques Marquette (1637–1675)

settled as a trading post in 1608 by French explorer Samuel de Champlain. It had been captured by the British in 1629 but was returned to France in 1632. It remained a colonial trading center until it was named the capital of New France from 1663 to 1763.

In less than a month after his arrival, Marquette found himself in all the wilderness he could want. It was the frontier **outpost** of Trois-Rivieres (Three Rivers), halfway between the cities of Quebec and Montreal. One of the oldest settlements in Canada, it was founded in 1634 by Samuel Champlain.

Almost from the beginning of his stay in North America, Marquette proved to be gifted in learning the different languages spoken by the various native peoples in the colony. Eventually, he conversed well in six Native American languages. His work was rewarded in a way in 1668 when he was sent to Sault Ste. Marie (Michigan and Ontario), the most difficult and dangerous **mission** in New France. It was started in 1660 by Father Menard, who disappeared into the Wisconsin forests. The mission was revived in 1665 by Father Allouez. This was the new home of the Huron as well as the not always friendly Ottawa, who had been driven by other Native Americans to the shores of Lake Huron.

The Ottawa were Algonquian-speaking people. The term *algonquin* refers to a dialect of the Ojibway people of Wisconsin and Canada. The Ottawa lived around northern Michigan and the Ottawa and French rivers in Canada. They were known as traders, canoeing as far east as Quebec to buy and sell merchandise. They lived in agricultural villages in summer and separated into family groups for winter hunts. Attacked by the Iroquois in the late 1600s, they scattered throughout lower Michigan and Wisconsin and northern Illinois.

The Huron, who lived basically along the St. Lawrence River, spoke Iroquois. They lived in villages and practiced agriculture. The Huron competed with their bitter enemies, the Iroquois, for the fur trade. They were nearly destroyed by Iroquois invasions in 1648–1650. Eventually, white settlers drove them from their lands in Ohio and Michigan and most migrated to Kansas and then to Oklahoma.

Marquette found a rather peaceful life among these Native Americans. The mission had been started in 1660 but died out before it was started again in 1665. The Native Americans were friendly to the new missionary and he converted many of them to Christianity. A year later, he moved on to the mission at La Pointe on the south shore of Lake Superior (now in Wisconsin). He spent eighteen months there meeting tribes from many areas, including the friendly Illinois peoples. They told Marquette that they had crossed a great river on their way to the mission. He thought that one day he would like to build a mission for these gentle people.

The Illinois were a confederation of Algonquian-speaking people living in what is now southern Wisconsin, northern Illinois, and parts of Missouri and Iowa. They were primarily hunters, although they did practice some agriculture. Harassment by northern groups forced the Illinois to concentrate along the Illinois River, but raids by the Iroquois weakened them and their population was greatly reduced. By 1832, their remaining lands had been sold, and the Illinois were forced to move to Kansas and then to Oklahoma.

Although groups such as the Illinois had friendly relationships with the early explorers, the Europeans unwittingly brought with them diseases like measles and smallpox that proved deadly to the Native Americans, who had no immunity to these foreign diseases. Across North America, native peoples died by the thousands after contact with their invaders.

Marquette enjoyed a more successful relationship with the Illinois than with the temperamental Ottawa and Hurons. However, when the Hurons abruptly left La Pointe after a fight with the fierce Sioux, Marquette followed them. The Sioux were also known as Dakota, or North American plains people. At

the middle of the 1600s, they lived primarily around Lake Superior, gathering rice and hunting. They lived in tepees, which is a Sioux word, and valued brave deeds in warfare. Of all the Plains people, the Sioux were most fearsome in resisting the advance of European invaders into their territory.

After Marquette followed the Huron, he founded the mission and trading post of Michilimackinac in the summer of 1671. Today, it is the town of St. Ignace, Michigan, on the Mackinac peninsula between Lake Huron and Lake Michigan. It was there, on December 8, 1672, that 34-year-old Father Marquette met a 26-

Today Colonial Michilimackinac Village is a historic park that attracts visitors from all over the world.

This statue depicts Louis Jolliet (1645–1700)

wilderness. Jolliet was baptized on September 21, 1645, in New France, probably in Beaupre, near Quebec City. His father was a craftsman who died when the boy was five years old. Louis's mother married again and they moved to the Isle of Orleans, but returned to Beaupre after her second husband drowned in 1665.

Young Louis was an exceptional student and entered Jesuit college in Quebec when he was 11 years old. He studied mathematics, logic, and the classics. He was also quite gifted in music, playing the organ at the cathedral in Quebec for many years. Jolliet also studied philosophy and prepared to enter the priesthood. He was such a good student that Bishop Francois de Laval of Quebec took a special interest in him. But as time went on, the young man had a change of heart. The priesthood was not really what he wanted. So, with the backing of Laval, he went to Europe in 1667 to continue his studies in science. One of his courses was hydrography, the study of bodies of water. He would find it useful later in life.

Jolliet returned to Canada in 1668 with all thoughts of the priesthood left behind. He would lead a life of adventure in the Canadian wilderness. With some money borrowed from Laval, he entered the fur trade, the main business in New France at the time. Once or twice over the next three years, Jolliet made an expedition west, often using Iroquois as guides.

year-old Canadian explorer named Louis Jolliet. The journey that followed put them both in the history books.

Jolliet the adventurer

Like Marquette, Canadian-born Louis Jolliet (1645–1700) had been educated for the priesthood. But he left the religious life for adventure in the Canadian

Many groups around the lower Great Lakes spoke the Iroquois language. In the 1600s and 1800s, the Iroquois league was a confederation of the Mohawk, Oneida, Onondaga, Cayuga, and Seneca peoples. For their sheer numbers, they were well respected by the French and English coming into the area to settle.

On one trip guided by the Iroquois, Jolliet and his party traveled down Lake Huron and into Lake Erie by way of the Detroit River. They were the first group in recorded history to do so. In June 1671, Jolliet was one of the signers of a document claiming that France was now in possession of the Great Lakes region. By now, Jolliet had become an expert at mapmaking and was probably more familiar with the wilderness around the Great Lakes than any other person in Canada at the time.

A year later, Jolliet was ready for the expedition of his career. More and more people in New France were talking about a great river. Explorers and settlers, borrowing a word from the native peoples, were calling it the Mississippi. If such a river actually existed, France certainly wanted to get there before England did. But where was it? Where did it flow? South to the Gulf of Mexico? Southwest to the Gulf of California? Who should lead such an important expedition?

In 1672, the governor-general of New France was a man with the rather grand-sounding name of Louis de Buade, Comte de Frontenac. He was egotistical, not always honest, hopelessly extravagant, and a bad manager. All he seemed to have going for him was charm, which then as now can be a powerful tool. And he also knew what he wanted, so he chose Louis Jolliet to lead the expedition. Jolliet was the obvious choice. He knew the Great Lakes region better than any other Canadian. He was smart, an expert mapmaker, and skilled at surviving in the wilderness.

Jolliet meets Marquette

Jolliet and his party left Quebec on October 4, arriving at St. Ignace in early December. There he met the priest in charge of the **mission,** Father Marquette. At the recommendation of the Jesuits in Quebec, the priest was chosen to accompany Jolliet in the search for the great river. He would preach to any native peoples they met along the way. Marquette, with a passionate interest in geography and a real desire to meet new native peoples, was delighted with his orders.

The two men spent the winter at the mission, making plans, drawing maps, talking endlessly about the forthcoming expedition. History usually speaks of "Marquette and Jolliet," as though the missionary were the leader, but it was actually Jolliet who was in command.

By May 17, 1673, they were ready. They left the **mission** with two canoes and five companions. The names of the five are unknown. The actual record of the expedition is thought to have been written by a Father Dablon, Marquette's Jesuit superior in the Great Lakes region. Marquette had sent him a record of his journal. That was a lucky or a smart thing to have done, because most of Jolliet's notes did not survive.

The great journey

In his notes Marquette recorded how they loaded the canoes with a lot of Indian corn and some smoked meat. Marquette and Jolliet had carefully planned the route of their journey. The priest also noted that they had drawn a crude map of the country they would explore, taken from what they were told by Native Americans.

The party traveled west along the north shore of Lake Michigan and then southwest to Green Bay, now in Wisconsin, arriving about the end of May. According to Marquette, they met the people of what he called the wild oats. He had previously preached to them and had converted a few to Christianity. What

Jolliet and Marquette travel with their crew on the big river.

Marquette called wild oats was wild rice, which grew naturally in the small rivers or bogs.

The people of the wild oats, although friendly, warned against the expedition's plan to explore the great river. They spoke of strangers who would kill without cause and of monsters on the river itself. They also said the river itself was rapid and dangerous and could easily capsize a canoe. Marquette and Jolliet thanked them for their advice and moved on.

From there, they entered the Fox River. At about the town of present-day Berlin, Wisconsin, they met some astonished Mascouten people. The Mascouten could not believe that seven men in just two canoes were taking such a dangerous journey. This was as far west as any Frenchman had explored. Mascouten guides led the way, and the party carried the canoes and supplies some 100 miles (161 kilometers) over-land to the Wisconsin River. Then the guides returned to their village, leaving the expedition alone in this strange land. After another trip of about 118 miles (190 kilometers), they arrived at what is now Prairie du Chien, where the Wisconsin River feeds into south-flowing waters.

The great river

On June 17, 1673, the party arrived. There it was, just as the Native Americans had said. They were looking at the river they had sought for so long. Marquette and Jolliet knew immediately that they had found it. Marquette gave it the grand-sounding name of "Riviere de la Conception." Eventually, it was just simpler to refer to it as the Native Americans did—Missi Sipi.

Happily, the party entered the river and paddled south. They were amazed by the great herds of buffalo and vast stretches of **prairie,** but they saw no signs of human life.

In fact, they saw no one until late in June when they noticed tracks along the riverbank. Pulling the canoes ashore, they followed a trail inland. It led to a Peoria village on the Iowa River. There was surprise and some nervous moments on both sides when Marquette and Jolliet showed up. However, some of the old men of the village lifted their pipes in the air, which the explorers took to be a friendly **gesture.** In fact, the Peoria were quite friendly and hospitable and fed them well.

The explorers stayed with the Peoria until the end of the month. Once again they canoed south, passing the joining of both the Missouri and Ohio Rivers. The Missouri alarmed them a good deal at first because its waters were so muddy and turbulent. In fact, the Missouri River is often called "Big Muddy," because its rough waters continually wash away so much soil.

About mid-July just above the mouth of the Arkansas River, north of the boundary between present-day Arkansas and Louisiana, the small expedition met another group of Native Americans.

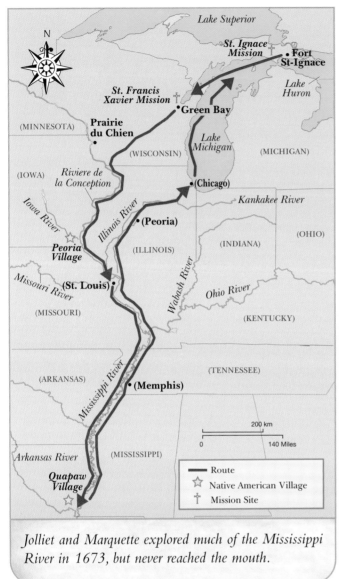

Jolliet and Marquette explored much of the Mississippi River in 1673, but never reached the mouth.

men. With great relief to the newcomers, the older men of the village arrived. They calmed everyone and told the intruders—as best they could—not to be afraid. The Quapaw spoke a language that Marquette could not understand.

Despite the uneasy atmosphere, Marquette and Jolliet spent a couple of days with the Quapaws. All in all they were treated well—at least by the older members of the group. The Quapaws told them that a trip to the mouth of the river would take them about ten days. Actually, it would have taken them much longer, for the Gulf of Mexico was some 700 miles (1,127 kilometers) to the south. Yet Jolliet and Marquette would surely have gone on had not the Quapaws given them another piece of news. They would have to pass through Spanish lands to reach the gulf. Since France and Spain were frequently at war during these early years, the explorers feared capture. So wiser heads prevailed. In late July the small party began its journey back home.

Thus, Marquette and Jolliet never saw the mouth of the Mississippi River, nor where the river began. Those discoveries were left to other explorers. However, both men were now convinced that the river flowed to the Gulf of Mexico and not to the west. They began their homeward journey satisfied that they had recorded much of this major river system.

These were the Quapaw, and, unlike the Peoria, they were decidedly unfriendly. In fact, they approached the two canoes with hatchets, bows, and arrows, looking very much like they intended to use them. For a few tense moments, the young Quapaw warriors circled the explorers, staring fiercely at these strange-looking

Not much is known about the trip home, except that it was largely uneventful. They returned by a different route, although it is not known why. This time they paddled up the Illinois River, which branches off the Mississippi north of St. Louis. From the Illinois, they carried the canoes—called portaging—to the site of present-day Chicago. Then they sailed up the shore of Lake Michigan to Green Bay where they stopped at the Saint Francis Xavier **mission.** It was mid-October, 1673. They had traveled more than 4,000 miles (6,437 kilometers) in 5 months.

The end of the team

After Jolliet rested for a few weeks, the soon-to-be-famous exploring team parted. Jolliet left for Montreal. Marquette, exhausted and sick from the journey, remained at the mission. He stayed there for a year getting back his strength and writing reports of his observations about the river. When he felt well enough, he set out on his long-held wish to build a mission for the Illinois tribe. With two companions, he departed in October 1674, but they were caught by an early winter. The small party camped near the site of present-day Chicago, becoming the first Europeans to live there. Some of the Illinois people visited them during the winter, and in the spring Marquette felt well enough to move on.

He reached the site of the Indian village, near present-day Utica, Illinois, in time for Easter. Marquette set up a new mission called the Immaculate Conception of the Blessed Virgin. But he knew that his health was failing and he wanted to return to St. Ignace. However, Marquette never made it. He died on May 18, 1675, on the eastern shore of Lake Michigan at the mouth of a river now called Pere Marquette, near present-day Ludington. It is said that before his death he thanked God for being allowed to die poor and in the wilderness as did Saint Francis Xavier.

Two years later, Marquette's remains were carried to the mission at St. Ignace and buried in the chapel. Some 200 years later, in 1877, his remains were unearthed and reburied. Fragments, however, were taken to Milwaukee, Wisconsin, and given to Marquette University, a Jesuit institution founded in 1857 and named for him. Also named for him are counties in Michigan and Wisconsin and a Michigan city on Lake Superior. There is also a statue of the gentle missionary in Washington, D.C.

When Jolliet left Father Marquette at Green Bay in late 1673, he spent the winter at Sault Ste. Marie in Upper Michigan. There he completed his journal as well as several maps of the Mississippi region. Unfortunately, they were all lost early in 1674 when Jolliet's canoe overturned in the **rapids** above Montreal on the homeward journey. He was later able to redraw several of the maps and reconstruct some of the papers from memory.

The adventurer settled down a bit after that. He became a fur merchant on the lower St. Lawrence River and married Claire-Francoise Byssot in 1675. They had several children. Jolliet wanted to establish a colony in the Illinois region on the Mississippi. However, the government of New France felt that it was already spreading its resources too thin over the region.

In 1679, Jolliet was called out of retirement and sent to scout an overland route to the rich fur-trading area of Hudson Bay. Leaving Quebec in April, he traveled to the south end of Hudson Bay and back. He found many English fur traders in the area and warned the New France officials that they would lose their hold on the trading business if the English were allowed to operate freely.

In return, Jolliet was given land on the lower St. Lawrence River, and he and his wife built their home on the island of Anticosti. He continued to be a successful fur trader, making several short expeditions, including one to the coast of Labrador in 1689. Three years later, he was named the official hydrographer of New France and taught at Quebec's Jesuit college. His last expedition began on April 28, 1694, when he sailed once again along the Labrador coast. He was the first to draw maps of the region. Jolliet returned to Quebec in October, dismayed to find that the British had taken over the island of Anticosti in his absence.

Louis Jolliet died of unknown causes in 1700. Through the years, his fame was somewhat overshadowed by Jacques Marquette, probably because the priest's journals were preserved. But together these two men opened the Great Lakes region and the Mississippi River Valley for future settlements, colonies, and, eventually, countries.

The St. Lawrence River links the Great Lakes to the Atlantic Ocean by way of the St. Lawrence Seaway.

Chapter Two

Rene-Robert Cavelier, Sieur de La Salle

France Enters Its Claim (1679–1687)

Rene-Robert Cavelier, **Sieur** de La Salle (1643–1687), dedicated explorer and adventurer, second son of a wealthy French family, stood at the mouth of the Mississippi River. The date was April 9, 1682. He held a sword in one hand and the flag of France in the other. There on the shores of the Gulf of Mexico, he claimed the river, its branches, and all the land touched by its waters. He did this in the name of his king, Louis XIV of France. And in the king's honor, La Salle called the region "Louisiana." It was many times the size of his native land.

This grand moment was the high point of La Salle's career. It was also a big step for France, which had dreams of becoming the major European power in North America. La Salle thought that this vast new territory would link French settlements along the St. Lawrence River in Canada with a new colony on the Gulf of Mexico. That never quite happened. Yet, for that moment and with that claim, La Salle set in motion the plans for a great French colonial empire.

Robert La Salle was an explorer who craved adventure more than gold. He saw himself as the builder of French power and prestige. Driven by the excitement of the unknown, he put all

A painting of Rene-Robert Cavelier (1643–1687)

his boundless, single-minded energy and determination into the work of exploring. Besides his travels on the Mississippi, he explored the Great Lakes region and may have been the first European to see the Ohio River. La Salle claimed that he was, but historians doubt the truth of his claim.

A restless youth

He was born Rene-Robert Cavelier in Rouen, France, on the Seine River about 70 miles (113 kilometers) west of Paris. Records show he was baptized in the parish church on November 22, 1643. His father was a wealthy merchant. "La

Salle," by which he is known, was the name of his family's country estate. He was tutored at home until he was about nine years old. Then he began classes at the local school run by the Jesuits, more formally known as the Society of Jesus. At his father's request, he went to Paris to study for the priesthood. His brother, Jean, was already a priest.

La Salle received a fine education under the demanding Jesuits and was especially good in science and mathematics. After taking his first vows in 1660, he enrolled at College Henri IV, near the city of Angers. But La Salle did not take well to the strict monastic life. It was too conservative and far too confining for his independent nature and restless energy. He was impatient, easily frustrated, unwilling to listen to advice other than his own. So, after his father's death when La Salle was 22, he left the priesthood to seek adventure. He also had to find some way to make a living. Since he had taken a vow of poverty as a priest, he could not expect any inheritance from his family.

Jean Cavelier was now a priest in Montreal, New France. The colony was growing. King Louis had made New France a province in 1663. That meant the colony would be governed from Quebec instead of from far away in France as it had been. Just as important was the fact that the French seemed to have tamed the Iroquois **Confederacy.** Five native peoples—the Mohawk, Oneida, Onondaga, Cayuga, and Sen-

eca— had united to give the French a good deal of resistance in the area. The conflict was over the rich fur trade. But for now at least, all seemed peaceful. It was a good time and place for La Salle. In addition, his brother could help him start a new life.

In the summer of 1666, La Salle sailed across the Atlantic. He did indeed get a new start. His brother's religious order, St. Sulpice, granted him some land on the western end of the island of Montreal. In return, he was to recruit settlers from France to build a colony. La Salle put up several buildings, became a farmer, began a fur trade with native peoples in the area, and became quite wealthy. His **outpost** was later called *La Chine,* which referred to his dream of developing a trade route to China through North America. La Salle also learned various local dialects and was quite boastful about this ability. It enabled him to listen to stories that Native Americans told about the region.

La Salle ran his fur trading business near Lachine **Rapids** for about two years. Then, during the winter of 1668–1669, he had an exciting conversation with members of the Seneca tribe. They spoke of a great south-flowing water that might be a route to the sea. Actually, the Native Americans spoke of two rivers. One they called the *Ohio,* meaning "beautiful water." The other was the *Missi Sipi,* or "big water." It was possible, thought La Salle, that the "big water" might lead west. It might be the long-

La Salle began his adventure in the city of Montreal.

sought Northwest Passage. So began his dream of finding the Mississippi River.

The search

Suddenly, the life of a landowner lost all interest for La Salle. Here was what he had longed for—a life of adventure. And now he had a definite goal. In the summer of 1669, he sold his land back to the St. Sulpice monastery and began his career as an explorer.

La Salle left Montreal on July 6 in the company of two priests of the St. Sulpice order. They were going to establish a **mission** to the west. With seven canoes, four of them belonging to La Salle, they paddled down the St. Lawrence River to the southern shore of Lake Ontario. Since La Salle was certain he could talk with the Native Americans, they went ashore to hire some of the Iroquois people as guides. He was somewhat upset to learn that none of the Iroquois could understand him. Setting out to the west again, they came to the mouth of the Niagara River and heard the noise of the great falls, which they did not see.

In a village at western Lake Ontario, La Salle and his companions met Louis Jolliet, who was returning from a trip in the northwest. At this point, La Salle parted with his priest companions, who decided to follow Jolliet's route. La Salle set out for the Ohio River, which he judged to be nearby.

No one knows exactly where La Salle traveled over the next two years, or what he saw. He later claimed that he found the Ohio River and sailed down to Louisville. That would make him the first European explorer on record to see the Ohio. Historians doubt this, however, and think that he saw it for the first time some ten years later.

Frontenac appears

Meanwhile, back in New France, a big change would lead La Salle to his dream. In 1672, Frontenac had been appointed governor-general for the province. He shared La Salle's dream of building French prestige and power in the New World. When the two men met, a bond was formed. Frontenac had the power in New France, La Salle had influence back home. Together, they would extend French military rule in the area, prevent the Dutch and English from getting control of the fur trade on the upper Great Lakes, and keep peace with the Iroquois. One might think that such a policy would please residents of New France. But the plan was strongly opposed by Montreal merchants, who were afraid their own fur trade would suffer, and by the missionaries, particularly the Jesuits, who feared losing influence with the Iroquois.

Nevertheless, within a year of his arrival in Quebec, the governor-general established Fort Frontenac (present-day Kingston), a fur-trading post on northeastern Lake Ontario, and made friends with the Iroquois. He sent Louis Jolliet to explore the Mississippi River and follow it to its mouth (see Chapter 1). When news reached New France that Marquette and Jolliet had explored the great river for much of its length, there was a rush to expand into the area.

In 1675, Frontenac sent La Salle back to France to see Louis XIV and get permission for a **monopoly** on the region's fur trade. Frontenac wrote to the king that Robert La Salle was "a man of intelligence and ability, more capable than anybody else I know here to accomplish every kind of enterprise and discovery." Louis was impressed enough with the message and the messenger to grant the monopoly and a title of nobility to La Salle.

La Salle sailed back to New France in the company of Father Louis Hennepin, who had joined him in explorations around the Great Lakes. The friar was the first to provide a written description of Niagara Falls. However, his claims about his travels were so exaggerated—including that he explored all the way to the mouth of the Mississippi—that his reports are not regarded as reliable.

Frontenac put La Salle in command of the new fort, and they made plans to extend the monopoly and explore farther west. Over the next three years, La Salle probably traveled around the upper Great Lakes and gained quite a fortune with his control of the fur trade.

La Salle asks Louis XIV for permission to explore the Mississippi.

But his restless nature caught up with him again. The unexplored lands to the west seemed much more attractive than the fur trade, no matter how profitable.

New explorations

So, it was back to France in 1677. This time King Louis XIV gave him permission to explore the vaguely defined territory called "western parts of New France." He was told to build forts wherever he thought necessary. In a generous mood, the king also granted a trade monopoly on buffalo hides and other furs—but not beaver. However, the king's generosity went only so far. Any explorations La Salle undertook were at his own expense.

The explorer returned to New France in 1678 in the company of a soldier of fortune named Henri de Tonti. Italian by birth, he became a trusted friend and La Salle's most valuable lieutenant. The most striking feature of Tonti's appearance was the velvet glove he usually wore to cover an iron claw that replaced his right hand. The hand had been blown off fighting the Spanish in Sicily.

With Tonti's help and the backing of Frontenac, La Salle was able to take over—illegally—a large part of the fur trade. He repeatedly ignored the king's restriction on beaver pelts, even after warnings from Louis himself. This made the Montreal fur traders furious.

To open the West for an expanding French empire, La Salle and Frontenac established a shipyard near Buffalo on the Niagara River. Under Tonti's direction, the 60-foot-long *Griffon* was constructed and launched in the early summer of 1679. A griffon is a mythical animal with the head and wings of an eagle and the body of a lion. It appeared on Frontenac's coat of arms and also decorated the prow of the ship.

The Fate of the Griffon

In August, the *Griffon* sailed into Lake Erie, becoming the first commercial vessel to do so. It continued into Lake Huron, then Lake Michigan, and eventually to Green Bay, Wisconsin. There it took on a great load of beaver, otter, and deer pelts. La Salle had sent Tonti ahead to gather the furs for pickup. With this profitable and quicker water route, La Salle hoped to finance his explorations of the Great Lakes and his search for the great river. He also hoped to enlarge the French empire.

Native peoples in the Green Bay area were not particularly happy to see the *Griffon* sail into view. They rightly saw the ship as a symbol of the growing power of the European newcomers in the region.

The *Griffon* was loaded with its valuable cargo and sent back to Niagara. The crew was supposed to empty the hold and return to Michilimackinac, where Lakes Michigan and Huron connect. Tonti would be waiting with about 20 men, whom La Salle had sent ahead to gather furs the previous winter. They would all get back on the *Griffon* and sail to the mouth of the St. Joseph River. There, La Salle and his 14 men would be waiting.

It did not quite work out that way. La Salle and his small party traveled

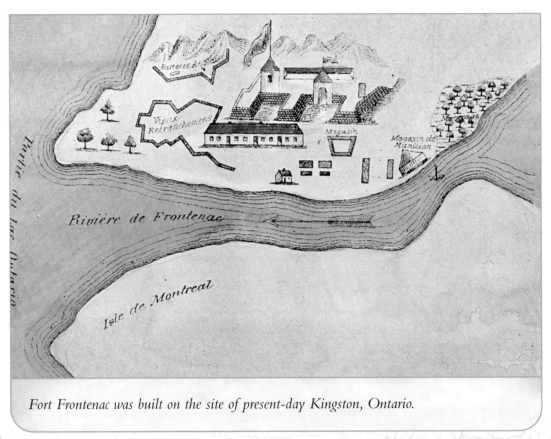

Fort Frontenac was built on the site of present-day Kingston, Ontario.

along the southeastern shore of Lake Michigan. In early December, they reached the mouth of the St. Joseph. Finally, Tonti and his crew appeared, but the *Griffon* did not. In fact, the ship, the men, and the cargo were never seen or heard from again. To this day, no one knows what happened to them.

With the winter snows increasing and his men showing signs of mutiny at being stuck in the wilderness, La Salle wisely decided to move on. Some say it was La Salle's own personality as much as the weather that was the problem. Not so much a leader, he was a dictator, rarely listening to anyone's advice.

The party, which now numbered 34, traveled along the St. Joseph and **portaged** their canoes overland to the Kankakee, which is a tributary of the Illinois River. By early January 1680, they had sailed down the Illinois to Lake Peoria, where La Salle built another fort. But he was greatly worried about the disappearance of the *Griffon*. That, coupled with the surliness of his men, may have caused him to name this new fort *Crevecoeur*, which is French for "heartbreak." It was, indeed, a low point in La Salle's dream of an empire.

The bitter trip back

By February La Salle could stand the waiting no longer. He sent Hennepin and two others to explore the upper Mississippi and start gathering furs once more. As it turned out, Hennepin never rejoined La Salle. He and his companions were captured by the Sioux, who took them on several hunting expeditions. On one of them, Hennepin reached the Falls of St. Antony. It is the site of what is now Minneapolis, Minnesota, a natural barrier that was to prevent later travel by barge. The friar was rescued by Daniel Greysolon, a French adventurer, in July 1680 and returned to France two years later. His overblown accounts of the journeys, particularly the importance of his own role, were soon discredited. Hennepin spent the rest of his life in obscurity until his death in Rome in about 1701.

A month after Hennepin left the fort, so did La Salle. Putting Tonti in charge with instructions to build another ship, La Salle headed back to Fort Frontenac on Lake Ontario. He had to find out about the *Griffon*. In addition, he was worried about money. As usual, he owed a good deal of it. Now he heard that his creditors were seizing supplies at Frontenac as payment. La Salle was determined to put a stop to that. He also needed more money for the new vessel and a new expedition.

Robert La Salle was a hard man to deal with, but he was no less hard on himself. His journey back to Fort Frontenac, which took only a little more than two months, has been called the most difficult ever made by Europeans in that region up to that time. Winter was ending, which only made conditions worse. The ground was a spongy mess of

The Mississippi River flows through Memphis, Tennessee.

mud, ice, and melting snow, and the route unknown and uncertain. He traveled up the Illinois River, around the top of Lake Michigan, and overland to Lake Erie. Sixty-five days and more than 1,000 miles (1,609 kilometers) later, he was back at Frontenac. The date was May 6, 1680.

Searching for Tonti

It was a disheartened La Salle who reached the fort. There was simply no news of the *Griffon*. It was lost. And to make matters worse, a letter from Tonti was waiting for him. The men at Fort Heartbreak had finally revolted. They had taken all they could carry, destroyed the fort, and run away. Only Tonti and five others remained.

La Salle had to get back to the fort to help his friend. But first he had to go to Montreal for more money. This took some time, and it was well into late autumn 1680 before he was ready to leave. The return expedition started out with 25 men. La Salle left 15 of them at Michilimackinac and continued his journey to the fort. Although Tonti's letter had warned him, the complete destruction was a shock. His frustration was even greater when he saw that Tonti and the five remaining loyal men had also disappeared.

In search of his trusted friend, La Salle traveled down the Illinois River to the Mississippi. There at last he saw the river he had been seeking for so long. But he could hardly linger to enjoy or explore it. Fearful for Tonti's safety, La Salle pushed on. But with winter coming and no trace of Tonti, a weary La Salle returned to Lake Michigan.

When the first signs of spring began to push through the snow, La Salle was ready to move again. Never defeated for too long, he had used the winter months to plan his trip down the Mississippi. He also tried to organize other native groups against the hostile Iroquois. It was acknowledged that the Iroquois were among the fiercest fighters. La Salle proposed a federation of native peoples against them, with himself as the leader. After he gained a tentative agreement among the various Native American groups, La Salle left for Michilimackinac.

The explorer reached the fort in June and to his delight, there was his old friend. Tonti had quite a tale to tell. He had been captured by the Iroquois but had escaped. After a dangerous journey up the Illinois to Lake Michigan and then Green Bay, he had finally reached Michilimackinac. Although he had endured much hardship through the months, Tonti said he was ready and eager for their next expedition.

The river at last

On December 21, 1681, La Salle, his crew of 25, including Tonti and 22 other Frenchmen, and a dozen small canoes left the mouth of the St. Joseph River for the Mississippi. Returning to Illinois country, they rebuilt their fort, this time on the upper Illinois River, near present-day Ottawa in La Salle County.

On February 6, 1682, at last La Salle lowered his canoes into the great waters of the Mississippi. There is no record of what he said when he finally saw the object of his long search, but he must have been overwhelmed by the sight of the great river that stretched endlessly before him. The long, deep, and wide Mississippi would eventually take La Salle to the Gulf of Mexico—the highlight of his life of exploration.

The next two months must have seemed easy by comparison with the years of getting there. On the journey downriver, he stopped at several Native American villages such as the Chickasaw at present-day Memphis, Tennessee; the Arkansas; and the Taensa on Lake St. Joseph in what is now Tensas parish in Louisiana. Although there were a few tense moments, most of the encounters were friendly. The Native Americans were generally curious about this band of strangers. Oddly, the very traits that annoyed La Salle's companions pleased the native peoples. His men found him stiff, serious, and stern. Native Americans regarded these characteristics as showing dignity and respect. Perhaps that is why La Salle completed his historic trip down the Mississippi without much incident in two months.

For the honor of France

The party arrived in the Mississippi **delta** on April 6. Over the next three days, La Salle split his group into three parts to explore the three **channels** of the river, which empty into the Gulf of Mexico. After they were reunited on April 9, La Salle took possession of all the river valley "in the name of the most high, mighty, invincible, and victorious Prince, Louis the Great, ... King of France." In name at least, he had given his native land a huge chunk of the North American continent.

Never again would Robert La Salle stand so high on top of his world. Now that he had claimed this vast region, he wanted to develop it. He proposed founding two colonies, one on the Gulf of Mexico, the other on the Illinois River to take care of the fur trade. In 1683, he built Fort St. Louis at Starved Rock on the Illinois. It is now a state park.

Then, La Salle ran into a brick wall in the form of the new governor-general of New France. His old friend and cohort Frontenac was replaced in 1682 by Joseph Antoine Lefebre, **Sieur** de la Barre, a favorite of the Jesuits and no friend to La Salle. The new governor not only turned down La Salle's request to build a colony in the delta, but he released the explorer from command of Fort St. Louis. Lefebre summoned La Salle to Quebec to answer for some of his questionable methods over the years.

La Salle claims the Mississippi River Valley for France.

The proud and stubborn La Salle was having none of the governor nor his request. He ignored Lefebre's summons and sent Tonti to turn over Fort St. Louis to the new commander. He did return to Canada, but instead of seeing the governor, he took a ship to France.

King Louis may have been displeased with La Salle in the past, but how could he be unhappy with the man who had just given him half a continent? Robert La Salle was a hero in Paris and in the royal court. He fascinated the king with his tales of the wonderful new and rich land he had delivered. To make his proposal for a colony more attractive, La Salle gave Louis a distorted map of the mouth of the Mississippi. It showed that the river entered the western side of the Gulf of Mexico rather than the eastern. This would put the proposed colony closer to Spanish holdings in Mexico. He told the king he would invade and capture some of the Spanish territory with 200 colonists and the aid—he assured the king—of 15,000 Native Americans. Some of the members of the royal court wondered if La Salle had lost his sanity.

But Louis was delighted. Any plan to harass the Spaniards, with whom France was currently at war, was top priority. Louis immediately returned all commands, property, and honors to the explorer. In addition, the king would, of course, be delighted to back La Salle's expedition.

The doomed colony

La Salle accepted the king's blessings. He was given the title of viceroy of North America and placed in command of all territory from Illinois to the Spanish-held borders in the south. To build a colony at the mouth of the Mississippi River, he was allotted a fleet of four ships, the 200 French colonists he requested, and many supplies.

But the expedition was doomed from the moment it set sail on July 24, 1684. A French naval officer named Tanguy de Beaujeu was put in charge of the four ships. He and La Salle fought constantly over leadership. Beaujeu was one of those who really did question whether the years of hardship in the wilderness had affected La Salle's mind. In fact, the explorer did suffer more and more from bouts of mental confusion in which he feared everyone was against him. At one point, he even suggested that loyal Tonti, who had not gone to France, had betrayed him.

In addition to the leadership conflict, the ships were attacked by pirates at sea. By the time they reached the West Indies, most of the crew were sick. La Salle was bedridden until November.

The final indignity occurred when the expedition left the West Indies but could not find the Mississippi! They ended up at Matagorda Bay in Texas, about 500 miles (805 kilometers) west of where they were supposed to be. Some say La Salle deliberately missed the

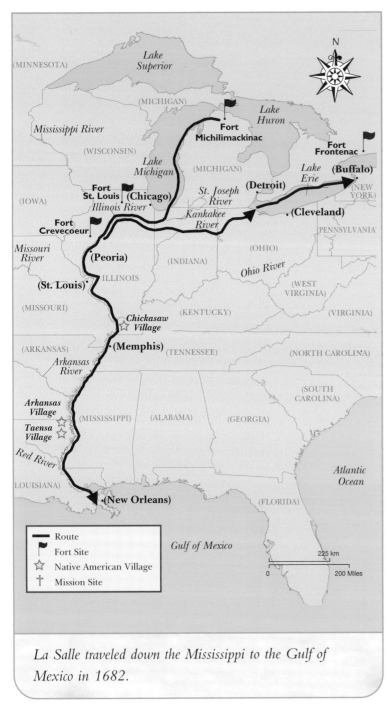

La Salle traveled down the Mississippi to the Gulf of Mexico in 1682.

mouth of the river to get closer to Spanish holdings. Others say he never knew the longitude of the mouth in the first place and simply could not find it again. Of course, in the late 1600s, navigation or directional devices on land and sea were very primitive by modern standards. The mouth of the Mississippi would not be located for another twelve years.

On March 12, 1685, the main ship carrying Beaujeu sailed back to France, leaving La Salle and the colonists behind. By this time, two ships had been wrecked and their supplies lost. Weakened by disease, hungry, and harassed by hostile Native Americans, the small, dejected band was expected to "hold for France a region large as half of Europe."

When Beaujeu returned to France, he asked the royal court to send help to the desperate colony. But Louis XIV was no longer in a generous mood. La Salle's dream had already cost more than he expected. The king refused.

While they awaited supplies that never arrived, La Salle tried to find the mouth of the Mississippi. He had the colonists build a large shelter and a fort, named St. Louis. It

An archaeologist works to raise La Salle's ship, the Belle.

was a backbreaking effort. Many were sick, and some died. By the time it was done, the mood of the colony of Fort St. Louis was as gloomy as their leader's.

From October until the following March, La Salle tried in vain to find the river. The last remaining ship, the *Belle,* was sunk and most of its crew drowned. Gone was any hope of getting help. Even so, the stubborn La Salle refused to give up. After another bout of illness, he devised a plan. If he could not find the river's mouth, at least he could be

sure he had found the Mississippi. He was sure he could do that by simply traveling to the northeast. At some point, he reasoned, he had to meet the river. Then, he would sail north to the Illinois and on to Montreal to get aid for the starving and frightened colony.

So it was that on April 22, 1686, La Salle took 20 men and left Fort St. Louis in charge of Henri Joutel, who would later write an account of the expedition. Although it is not known how far La Salle traveled, by August he was back,

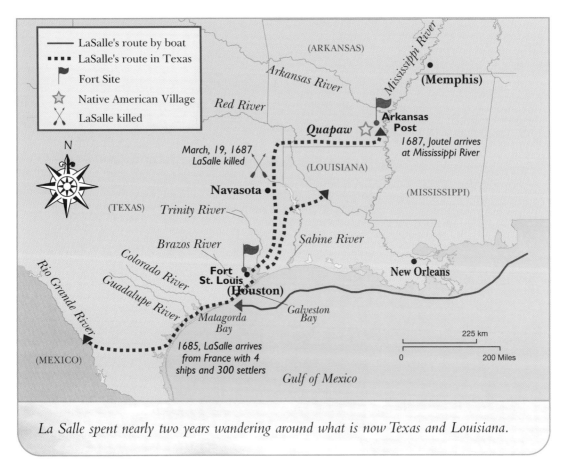

La Salle spent nearly two years wandering around what is now Texas and Louisiana.

a tired and dejected man. Only 8 men returned with him. Fever, alligators, disease, and hunger had taken the rest. And only 40 colonists remained.

La Salle well knew that their only hope was to try again. But he was not well enough to do so until January 1687. This time he took sixteen men with him. About mid-March, they reached present-day Navasota, Texas, northeast of present-day Houston. There a fight broke out between La Salle's nephew, Crevel de Moranget, and two of the colonists.

That night, the colonists murdered Moranget. Fearing a charge of murder and mutiny, on March 19, 1687, they also shot and killed Robert La Salle. His body was left for scavengers. Most of the remaining colonists were captured by the Spanish or killed by Native Americans. Joutel and a few others fled north and finally made it to safety in Montreal.

His friend Tonti called La Salle "one of the greatest men of the age." Frontenac admired his proud and unwavering spirit. Joutel wrote of his determination and courage, but also of his arrogance toward those who served him. It was that arrogance, according to Joutel, that caused his death.

Robert La Salle was a cold and forbidding man who seemed to have no passion except for his dream of a magnificent French empire. He was never popular or acknowledged as a heroic leader. He was never rewarded with an abundance of riches or glory in his lifetime. But history views him as a great explorer for his ceaseless energy and dedication toward his single goal. If France never built the empire of his dreams, it was not because Robert La Salle lacked the courage or the vision to keep trying.

Matagorda Bay on the Gulf of Mexico is about 80 miles (130 kilometers) east of Corpus Christi, Texas.

A postscript

In 1995, La Salle's sunken ship *Belle* was found in Matagorda Bay on the Gulf of Mexico. The Texas State Historical Commission immediately began plans for a multimillion-dollar recovery effort called the La Salle Shipwreck Project. Archaeologists who located the vessel said it was one of the most important shipwrecks ever found in North America.

The ship was discovered under about 12 feet (4 meters) of sand and silt in the bay midway between Galveston and Port O'Conner, Texas. About 20 percent of the hull was intact.

The project, which lasted until April 1997, uncovered cannon, boxes of muskets, pewter plates and cookware, and numerous other items. All artifacts were transported to Texas A&M University for conservation and display.

Chapter Three
Pierre Le Moyne d'Iberville
Where the River Ends (1686–1707)

A portrait of Pierre Le Moyne d'Iberville, who lived from 1661–1706

Pierre Le Moyne d'Iberville (1661–1706) has a distinction that sets him apart from other Canadian explorers. He is often regarded as Canada's first true hero. In the rugged, largely unexplored land that was called New France in the 1600s and 1700s, toughness and courage were much admired. A man might be uneducated, poor, even cruel and ruthless, but if he could stand up to the rigors of this harsh country, his name was praised.

Iberville was neither an uneducated nor a poor man. He was, however, sometimes cruel and ruthless in his military **exploits** and his handling of native peoples. Yet there is no question that, in toughness and courage, Iberville proved his worth many times over. His military campaigns took him to northern Canada as far as Hudson Bay, and he established a French colony at the mouth of the Mississippi.

Throughout his life, Iberville never wavered from his main reason for exploring North America: driving out the British to secure the continent for the French empire. His greatest military feats took place in Hudson Bay. His greatest service to France was in securing its claim to Louisiana.

More soldier than explorer
Iberville was born in New France in the Ville Marie section of Montreal in 1661. Pierre was the third of eight sons—and the most illustrious—born to Catherine Tierry and Charles Le Moyne, a wealthy fur trader who had emigrated to New France twenty years earlier. At the age of fourteen, Iberville joined the French navy. He learned to hate the British early on by taking part in raids against English

trading posts on Hudson Bay in the north. During this ten-year period, King Louis XIV was trying to expand and improve the French navy. When Iberville returned to Montreal in 1685, the young sailor was a naval officer and filled with glorious ideas of French expansion in North America.

In 1686, 24-year-old Iberville became a hero. Along with two of his brothers, he joined the expedition of Pierre de Troyes. The purpose was to drive the British from their posts on James Bay, which is the southern extension of Hudson Bay. There Iberville proved his innate toughness and courage.

Technically, France and England were not even at war in 1686. But there was trouble, certainly as the French saw it. Years earlier, in 1670, the British had incorporated the Hudson's Bay Company. Its purposes were to find a northwest passage to the Pacific Ocean, to settle adjacent lands, and to conduct any profitable business in the area. That turned out to be the fur trade, at which the British were very successful. The French had their own ideas about who should control the region.

In March 1686, Iberville and his brothers left Montreal with the de Troyes expedition on a perilous journey, even compared to the primitive traveling conditions of the time. They tramped some 600 miles (966 kilometers) along the Ottawa River on snowshoes. Then they built canoes and paddled down the Moose River for another 300 miles (483 kilo-

meters) into James Bay. It was only after 900 miles (1,448 kilometers) of travel that they could get ready to fight.

Iberville led the attacks on three British **outposts** in the bay. While storming Fort Moose, he got so far ahead of his own troops that he was cut off. Once he was inside the fort, the British swiftly closed the gates again, leaving Iberville's men outside. With just a sword in one hand and a pistol in the other, he managed to hold off the entire English force until his own troops broke down the gates. For that deed, he was made governor of the three trading posts. The adventurers returned to Montreal with a fur load worth a lot of money, in fact, the entire work of the Hudson's Bay Company for the year.

For the next ten years, the two sides carried on their own war. The British took back the forts; Iberville raided them again. He was determined to keep England from gaining the upper hand in North America. Iberville was a serious thorn in the side of the British in Canada.

King William's War

These back-and-forth raids were conducted without a declared war. That changed in 1689. William III of Britain, the provinces of the Netherlands, and the Austrian Hapsburgs began a war against Louis XIV and France. In Europe, it was called the War of the Grand **Alliance.** It was fought mainly over the French threat to expand their power. In North America, colonists in Canada and New England teamed up on the side of their respective

35

native countries. Their fight was called King William's War (1689–1697).

The British captured Port Royal in Acadia (today, the city of Annapolis in northwestern Nova Scotia) but could not take Quebec. The French fought in New York, New Hampshire, and Maine, but failed to take the big prize—Boston.

In 1690, Iberville led a campaign against Corlaer (now Schenectady, New York). An entire English settlement was pillaged and burned and 60 inhabitants were massacred. Iberville's hatred of the British was in full force and so was his reputation. In 1692 he failed to take Fort Pemaquid on the coast of Maine. Four years later he went back and burned it to the ground. This was followed by a raid against the fortified English settlement of St. John's in Newfoundland.

As soon as St. John's had fallen, Iberville led his men down the coast of Newfoundland, destroying English settlements as they went. As soon as the raiders passed, the English rebuilt their settlements and fisheries.

At one point, Iberville came up with a plan to attack New York City. He was nearly successful in taking it from the British. Iberville was a brilliant naval commander, noted for swift attacks and daring raids. In one outstanding battle, he commanded a small man-of-war called the *Pelican*. Facing three British warships, he sank the British ship *Hampshire*, sending all its crew to the bottom, and captured two other vessels. When his own

The French and Native Americans attack Schenectady, New York in 1690, during King William's War.

ship was struck and sinking, he was forced to abandon it. Leading his men ashore in hostile territory, he attacked the strongest English garrison in the area, Fort Nelson. The fort surrendered, but not before one of his brothers was killed and the youngest, Bienville, was badly wounded.

Overall, Iberville's campaigns as part of King William's War made him the most celebrated hero of New France. He was 36 years old and a married man. In 1693, he had wed Marie Therese Pollet de la Comte Pocatiere in Quebec.

After the *Pelican* battle, Iberville left for France to be honored at the royal court. He would never see Hudson Bay again. King William's War ended with the Treaty of Ryswick (or Rijswijk) in 1697. It settled the quarrel over Hudson Bay largely by restoring conditions to exactly what they were before the war. The resolution, however, was only temporary.

The French in Louisiana

The treaty that ended King William's War also seemed to end Iberville's career. He had spent almost his whole life fighting the British. Yet, for all his work, France was no closer to controlling the North than it was before.

But the royal court had a plan. The king was very impressed with Iberville's military genius. Why not put it to work elsewhere? Here was the perfect man to send to Louisiana! Ironically, it would be Louisiana, not his **exploits** in Hudson Bay, that would bring lasting fame to Pierre Iberville.

The vast territory called Louisiana had been claimed for France by Robert La Salle in 1682. Now, Louis XIV wanted Iberville to find and fortify the mouth of the Mississippi River so that other nations—really meaning England—could not try to take the region. Specifically, Iberville was told to locate a site at the river mouth that could be defended with "just a few men." He was given orders to establish a French colony, which La Salle had failed to do thirteen years earlier.

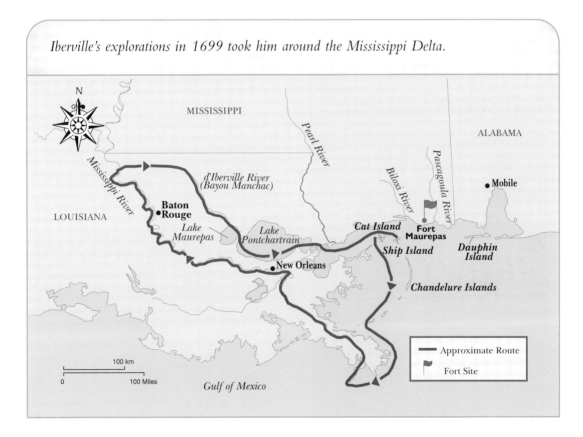

Iberville's explorations in 1699 took him around the Mississippi Delta.

One career ended, another began. The naval hero left Brest, France, in October 1698, for North America. His fleet consisted of the *Badine*, the *Marin*, two smaller vessels, and about 200 would-be colonists. Also on the voyage were two of Iberville's brothers, Sauvole and Bienville.

Iberville and his fleet arrived first in St. Domingue (now Santo Domingo, Dominican Republic). In January 1699, he sailed north to Florida and then along the Gulf of Mexico coast, passing the Spanish settlement at Pensacola. He sailed into and named Mobile Bay, an inlet of

A painting of King Louis XIV of France

the gulf on the coast of Alabama. Iberville and his men took some time to look around the area. After exploring a small island at the mouth of the bay that was covered with human bones, Iberville named it Massacre Island. It is now known by the less grizzly name of Dauphin Island.

The naval hero-turned-explorer sailed on, naming Cat Island and Ship Island off the coast of present-day Mississippi. But Iberville was well aware that, years before, La Salle had missed the mouth of the river. So he left the colonists and the two larger ships at Ship Island, sailing on the smaller vessels so he could get closer to shore in his search.

Early in March, a storm drove the exploring party, which consisted of Iberville, Bienville, and 48 others, into the **delta** of the Mississippi. At least Iberville thought he had reached the Mississippi. He could not be sure.

Cautiously, he sailed upriver where he reached a Bayagoula village. These people were friendly and entertained the strangers with a feast. The chief was wearing a blue cloak that Henri de Tonti, La Salle's second in command, had given to him on that failed expedition.

Iberville made some entries in his journal about the Bayagoula people. He described temples that these Native Americans had built, and in one entry, described a red pole that he said marked the boundary between the land of the Bayagoula and that of the Houma tribes. Although this is questioned by historians, it is interesting because "red pole" in French is *baton rouge*, the name of today's capital of Louisiana.

After seeing the blue cloak worn by the Bayagoula chief, Iberville was fairly sure he had found the right river. Some reports say he sailed up the Mississippi for another 200 miles (322 kilometers), but that is uncertain. He did sail back down to the mouth. On the way to the gulf, Iberville was the first European to see the 600-square-mile (1,554-square-kilometer) lake he named Pontchartrain in honor of the head of the French navy.

After this exploring tour of about six weeks, Iberville returned to Ship Island for the stranded colonists. One of his two larger ships had already returned to France. Iberville had to establish a permanent colony quickly before the other ship left, since the colonists would have no way to transport the cannon and other equipment they had brought.

The choice of the first permanent French settlement in French Louisiana could not have been more unwise. Iberville took the colonists to the mainland where they established Fort Maurepas or Old Biloxi (now Ocean Springs, Mississippi). The fort had 12 cannon and was fenced in by a nine-foot (three-meter) palisade. But the ground was barren sand. Agriculture was impossible. The freshwater supply was scarce. Besides that, the heat was unbearable. They would have been far better off inland with an ample water source, some shade, and good soil for growing

Today Lake Pontchartrain is a major recreational center.

crops. But Iberville was afraid of attack by Native Americans farther inland, and he believed the colony would prosper as near the river mouth as possible. He was wrong.

The second and third voyages

After the fort was built, Iberville sailed for France, leaving Sauvole in charge and 18-year-old Bienville as second in command. King Louis was probably happy to see Iberville, but he was more anxious to protect his first fragile French settlement. So, Iberville was soon back on the high seas. He returned to the Gulf of Mexico in early 1700.

It was a good thing he arrived when he did. Iberville was shocked to find that only 150 colonists and soldiers remained. Disease, fever, and starvation had weakened the colony. Iberville brought needed supplies and about 60 new settlers. He also had instructions to find out if silk could profitably be grown in the colony. It could not.

On this trip, Iberville built Fort La Boulaye, on higher ground than Biloxi, and about 40 miles (64 kilometers) south of what is now New Orleans. Before returning to France, Iberville explored the area of the lower Mississippi Valley. What he saw impressed him so much that he was determined the French must hold on to this land at all cost.

Iberville returned to France in May 1700, again leaving his brothers in charge. Soon after he left, the settlement at Biloxi was visited by the Spanish governor of Pensacola. He protested French settlements in the area, claiming that the entire gulf shore belonged to Spain. It

Native Americans grow sick from diseases carried by the Europeans.

was only a veiled threat, but suddenly France seemed to have another enemy in Louisiana besides the British.

Back in France, Iberville and the royal court were having a tug of war. The court wanted all possessions east and west of Louisiana to be taken by the French. That would include Spanish America. Iberville was always more interested in defeating the British. To that end, he wanted more settlers, more supplies, and more cannon.

Iberville returned to his colony for the last time in December 1701. A fever **epidemic** had taken the lives of many of the colonists during the year, including that of his brother Sauvole.

Fever and the quick spread of disease were always a grave threat to the early colonies. This was true even in Europe, but on the frontier where living conditions were generally far from sanitary and medical help was limited, the situation was much more grave. In addition, diseases such as smallpox or measles, which the explorers and settlers carried with them to the New World, were deadly to Native Americans. Never having been exposed to these illnesses, Native Americans in North America died by the thousands after the invasion from Europe began.

Young Bienville was now in command of the colony. Iberville was forced to admit that both colonies at Biloxi and La Boulaye were in bad condition. Agriculture was a total failure. So it was decided to abandon the Biloxi colony and move to a better site on Mobile Bay. Then, Iberville returned to France.

Back to the military

After the third expedition, Iberville never saw Louisiana again. He had planned another trip but bad health kept him in France. He did recover enough to take part in a military campaign against the British one more time.

The campaign was part of the War of the Spanish Succession (1701–1714). It turned Iberville's attention from colonizing Louisiana back to his first love—fighting the British.

This war began over who would sit on the Spanish throne after the death of Charles II, last of the Habsburg Spanish royal family. Also known as Charles the Mad for his recurring mental problems, the king had no children. At his death, Charles left all Spanish possessions to Philip, grandson of Louis XIV of France. Charles was convinced that only France had the military power to keep Spanish lands intact. Not happy with that choice, England formed an anti-French **alliance** with the Dutch Republic and other countries. When England's William III died in 1702, his successor, Queen Anne, vigorously kept up the war. A leading figure in her government was John Churchill, duke of Marlborough. He played such an important part in the conflict that it is also known as Marlborough's War.

Given the chance to fight his old enemy once again, Iberville was eager to return to active duty with the French navy. His youngest brother was still in charge of the Louisiana colony. In early 1706, Iberville went to the West Indies, leading a twelve-ship squadron whose purpose was to destroy Britain's hold on the region.

Once again attacking in the daring and swift raids that marked his naval career, Iberville sacked the islands of Nevis and St. Christopher. He forced the English to surrender 24 ships. In addition, he captured 1,700 settlers and 6,000 slaves. Iberville sailed on to Cuba, where he died on July 9, 1706, perhaps from yellow fever.

Iberville's were the first permanent settlements along the Gulf of Mexico, in what are now Alabama, Mississippi, and Louisiana. He established French control and sovereignty over the lower Mississippi Valley. He was the first European to reach the mouth of the Mississippi from the Gulf of Mexico, giving France another trade route.

Iberville died eight years before the end of the War of the Spanish Succession. It was settled by the Treaty of Utrecht in 1714. Had he lived, this adventurer would have been most unhappy to see Britain's rise to power in North America as well as Europe, at the expense of both Spain and France. Pierre Iberville was a ruthless, even cruel, man. He was also daring and courageous. His greatest dream was to turn over an entire continent to his beloved France. He very nearly succeeded.

Chapter Four
Jean-Baptiste Le Moyne de Bienville:
The Road to New Orleans (1696–1743)

It is often difficult to grow up in the shadow of an older, more famous sibling. Such was the fate of Jean-Baptiste Le Moyne de Bienville (1680–1767), youngest brother of Pierre Le Moyne d'Iberville. Less daring perhaps, less colorful, Bienville was in his way as loyal to his king and to the glory of France as was his more illustrious brother. Nineteen years younger than Iberville, he was given the thankless and nearly impossible task of maintaining French Louisiana against the growing forces of both England and Spain.

Bienville was not perhaps the most talented of leaders, but his resolve and loyalty were unquestioned. Ironically, his greatest claim to fame remains in full view for all to see, whereas his brother's deeds are largely remembered between the pages of a book. Bienville is the founder of New Orleans, the vibrant, charming, and colorful city of the South that has retained the flavor of his native land through the centuries.

Following in footsteps

The eighth and last son of Catherine Tierry and Charles Le Moyne of Montreal, New France, was born on February 23, 1680. Both parents died when he was young, and he was raised by his brother Charles, Baron de

Portrait of Jean Baptiste Le Moyne de Bienville (1680–1767)

Longueuil. When he was eleven years old, his brother Francois, **Sieur** de Bienville, was killed fighting the Iroquis. The Bienville title went to Jean-Baptiste.

Young Bienville grew up adoring his eldest brother, Pierre Iberville. And like most young boys, he longed to follow in his idol's footsteps. So, at the age of twelve, Bienville became a midshipman in the French navy. He was allowed to serve on Iberville's ship. He took part in raids against the British trading posts on Hudson Bay during the last years of King William's War (1689–1697). The conflict pitted England and other European forces against France and spilled over into North America. On September 5, 1697, Bienville served with his brother on the frigate *Pelican*. He was seriously wounded in the battle in which Iberville, in command, routed the British.

In French Louisiana

When the war ended with the Treaty of Ryswick, Bienville sailed with his brother to rediscover the mouth of the Mississippi River and establish a French colony there. The expedition left Brest, France, on October 24, 1698, with four ships and some 200 colonists. Bienville was just 18 years old.

The expedition reached the Gulf of Mexico in early 1699, and young Bienville proved himself quite useful. He had a flair for picking up foreign languages very quickly. This was of great help when the explorer ran into Native Americans. He was also a calm **mediator** when disputes arose among the colonists or between the Europeans and the Native Americans.

Bienville was with Iberville when they found the mouth of the Mississippi. He was also with Iberville when they saw the blue cloak in the village of the Bayagoulas. But when Iberville started back down the river, Bienville split off from him and took a different route. He had heard that a chief near the mouth of the river had a letter, which was referred to as "speaking bark." Supposedly it was left by Tonti, La Salle's second in command many years before. That would indeed prove that the Frenchmen had been on the Mississippi. Near the **delta,** Bienville did see the letter. The Native American who had saved it said that Tonti had made him promise to give it to the first Frenchman he met.

After the settlement at Old Biloxi, Iberville left for France. His brother Sauvole was put in charge of the colony with Bienville as second in command. During Iberville's absence, Bienville explored the lower reaches of the great river. Once he encountered a British vessel of at least 12 guns in the area still known as English Turn, about 18 miles (29 kilometers) south of New Orleans.

The captain's name was Barr and Bienville had already met him in Hudson Bay. Captain Barr said he was supposed to explore the mouth of the Mississippi and try to find an interior passage. Bienville is said to have explained that the French had already claimed the area. Whether Barr believed him or not, the British left without incident. The captain did, however, hint that he might be back.

During the spring of March to May 1700, Bienville also explored the Red River as far as present-day Natchitoches, Louisiana. The Red River, which is some 1,270 miles (2,044 kilometers) long, rises in New Mexico, flows southeast across Texas, and enters Louisiana north of what is now the city of Baton Rouge. There, the river flows into the Mississippi **delta,** emptying mainly into the Atchafalaya River.

On this exploring expedition, Bienville made **alliances** with many of the Native American groups in the area, hoping to ensure the safety of the little French colony.

Commander in chief

Bienville's brother Sauvole died of the fever that swept the Louisiana colony before Iberville's return late in 1701. Bienville was now in complete charge. Iberville brought with him a commission that made his youngest brother a king's lieutenant.

Bienville told his brother of his desire to move the colony to a more suitable location. Accordingly, in 1702, the old colony was moved to Fort Louis on Mobile Bay. Iberville returned to France, never to visit Louisiana again. At last, Bienville was out of the shadow of

The Red River flows near Natchitoches, Louisiana.

his eldest brother. And when Iberville died of yellow fever in Cuba in 1706, Bienville was now the authority in French Louisiana. In 1711, Bienville once again moved the colony, this time to present-day Mobile, Alabama.

Although Bienville worked hard to preserve the colony and keep peace with the surrounding Native Americans, the French settlement gradually declined after Iberville's death. Bienville was an able administrator, but he had enemies from within the colony and back in France. In fact, at one point Nicolas de La Salle, the commissary in France, sent a replacement to head the colony. But the replacement died en route, and Bienville kept his job.

He kept it until 1712. At that time, the French king granted the territory of Louisiana to a company that sent over a new governor. He was Antoine Laumet de Lamothe Cadillac and he served for three years, from 1713 to 1716. Bienville became second in command.

In the beginning Bienville and the new governor of the colony got along very well. So well, in fact, that Bienville considered marrying the governor's daughter. But the two men disagreed

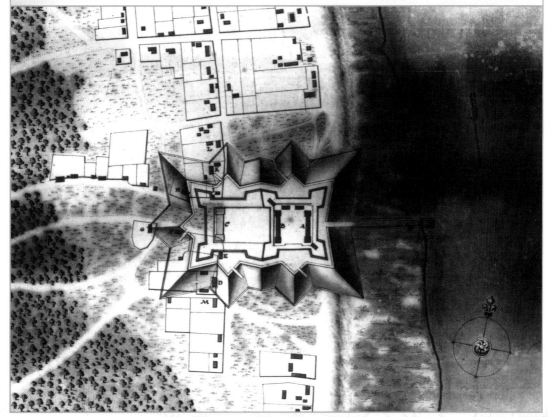

A sketch of Fort Louis, near present-day Mobile, Alabama

A member of the Natchez tribe

In 1716, on orders from Cadillac, Bienville led a military campaign against the Natchez people. At the time of the first French settlement, the Natchez numbered about 6,000 living in villages near the site of present-day Natchez, Mississippi. The Natchez and the French were friendly at first, but their relationship broke down, resulting in three wars, the first in 1716. Bienville succeeded in driving the Natchez from their villages. He established Fort Rosalie at what is now the city of Natchez.

Cadillac's term as governor was over in 1716, and Bienville hoped he would be appointed, but another governor arrived. The company that ran French Louisiana was dissolved the following year. The governor returned to France, and the territory came under the Company of the Indies, which specialized in colonization. It was headed by financier John Law. He gave the governor's post to Bienville.

The birth of New Orleans

If there ever was an easy time to administer the French colony in Louisiana, this was not it. Suddenly, great groups of colonists flooded into the area, lured by concessions that the company granted to noblemen. Bienville felt it was time to realize his dream of changing the location of the colony. He had his eye on a site that was right on the Mississippi, south of Lake Pontchartrain. When Law's company suggested establishing a port that would be a center for future trade upriver,

over many administrative matters, and the marriage never took place.

As Cadillac's deputy, Bienville explored much of the region around the Mobile colony and in the southern Louisiana territory. In 1714, his travels took him along the Alabama River. He built Fort Toulouse where the Coosa and Tallapoosa Rivers meet. The area later became an important fur-trading center.

Bienville told them of his idea. They agreed and left the actual founding of the city to him.

The city of New Orleans was named for a member of the French royal family, the Duc d'Orleans. It was laid out by Bienville in 1718. A year later, Spain and France were at war again. This was the War of the Quadruple **Alliance,** with Britain, the Dutch Republic, Austria, and France teamed up against Spain. They were trying to prevent the Spanish from changing the terms of the Treaty of Utrecht, which supposedly ended the War of the Spanish Succession. During the fighting in North America, Bienville returned to his military duties and twice captured Spanish-held Pensacola.

The troubles begin

In 1722, Bienville was pleased to have New Orleans become the capital of French Louisiana. Soon, however, he enacted a strict law that casts him in the role of inhumane dictator. He instituted the so-called Black Code, which harshly

An oil painting shows how the city of New Orleans looked in the 1800s.

regulated the conduct of African slaves. Numerous restrictions kept social control. Black people could not leave their homes without their owner's permission, were forbidden to learn to read or write, could not own firearms, and could not assemble except in the presence of a white person. Whipping, branding, imprisonment, and restraint were common forms of punishment. Death was imposed only in extreme cases, since slaves were considered valuable property.

That was only the beginning of Bienville's troubles as commandant of the capital. In 1723, he went back to fighting the Natchez. This time he did not have the support of the Company of the Indies. Charged with poor **administration** and plagued by internal conflicts with the colonists, Bienville was fair game for his enemies. He was called back to the French court in 1724 and charged with a lack of competence. However, Bienville staunchly defended his administration and detailed the harsh realities and difficulties of life on the frontier of North America. Nevertheless, he was dismissed from his post. For the first time since the French settled in Louisiana, a member of the Le Moyne family was not in charge.

Deprived of his office and publicly disgraced, Bienville settled down to a quiet life in Paris. That interlude lasted nearly a decade.

The recall

The Company of the Indies continued to govern Louisiana until 1731. But the job was poorly done. By that time there was so much trouble with the Natchez and the colony was in such financial ruin that the royal court took over. Bienville was urged to return. In 1733, he was back in New Orleans as the royal governor. The return, as he later remarked, gave him great joy and satisfaction.

Bienville's recall to Louisiana lasted for a decade. It was plagued by difficulty. Most troublesome were the continuing wars with Native Americans. During these conflicts between the French and the Natchez, in 1716, 1723, and 1729, some 400 Natchez were captured and sold into the West Indian slave trade. The remainder took refuge with the Chickasaw and later with the Cherokee. When the French demanded that the Chickasaw give up the Natchez, they refused. In fact, the Chickasaw refused any dealings with the French, and began to side with the British.

In response, Bienville led a military force of about 600 French soldiers against the Chickasaw in 1736. Heading north along the Tombigbee River, he planned to join another French force that was coming down the Mississippi. Instead, both forces were defeated, Bienville had to retreat, and some 20

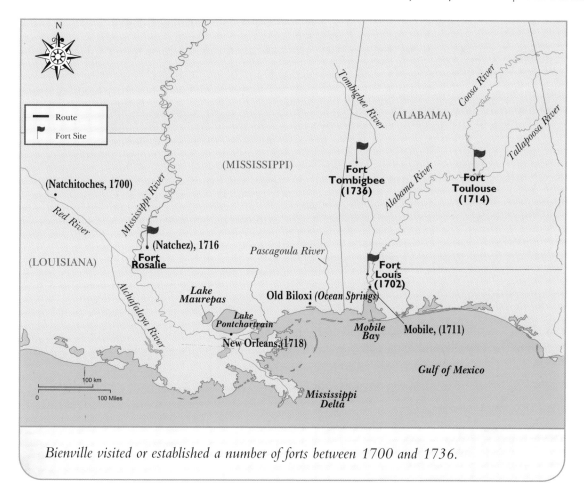

Bienville visited or established a number of forts between 1700 and 1736.

Frenchmen were burned at the stake. During this operation, Fort Tombigbee in central Alabama was established.

Another expedition was planned in 1739. A French military group from Canada met Bienville and his men near present-day Memphis, Tennessee. They were able to establish peace with the Chickasaw, but it was an uneasy peace since neither side trusted the other.

The last years

Bienville was worn out from the pressures of fighting the Natchez and Chickasaw and trying to solve the never-ending difficulties of the colony. So, he requested that the royal court accept his resignation, which it did. He left Louisiana on May 10, 1743, returning to private life in Paris.

Through all his years as a private citizen, Bienville never lost interest in his colony across the sea. So, it was with great sorrow that he heard France would cede the Louisiana territory to Spain. This was the result of the struggle for control over North America known as the French and Indian War

(1754–1763), part of the Seven Years' War in Europe. Bienville spoke eloquently before the court against giving up the territory and against his old enemy. It was no use. In 1763, by the Treaty of Paris, New Orleans and the Louisiana territory west of the Mississippi came under Spanish control. France also gave nearly all its remaining possessions in North America to Great Britain.

The citizens of New Orleans staged a brief rebellion, but it was quickly suppressed. Actually, New Orleans prospered under Spanish control and even began a brisk trade with the British despite the restrictions.

Bienville died in Paris on March 7, 1767. Had he lived another 33 years, he would have seen his beloved New Orleans in French hands once more. Napoleon Bonaparte was the leader of France in 1800. He was strong enough to convince the Spanish king, Charles IV, that the Louisiana territory should be returned as well. That meant the return of New Orleans and the mouth of the Mississippi.

Jean-Baptiste Le Moyne de Bienville perhaps had faced a hopeless task. He tried to carry on warfare and at the same time govern a frontier colony with little backing or support from the home country. But he did help to clear the way for the French into Alabama, Arkansas, and Tennessee. He built a number of settlements for France along the Mississippi Gulf coast. However, his claim to fame rests on the prize jewel of New Orleans.

A postscript

Bienville's New Orleans did indeed become a prize jewel. In 1803, Napoleon sold the Louisiana territory, including the port city, to the United States. There were a number of reasons for what seems a fantastic sale. Another war looming with Great Britain and the fact that France was very short of money are two of the main ones. The transfer of the Louisiana territory, which immediately doubled the size of the United States, took place in the main square of New Orleans, the Place d'Armes (now Jackson Square).

When New Orleans became part of the United States, it had a population of about 8,000 people, including 2,700 slaves. In the War of 1812, the British threatened to invade the city from the Gulf of Mexico. General (later president) Andrew Jackson scored a major victory against the British on January 8, 1815, not knowing the war had already ended.

For the next half century, New Orleans was a great cotton port. Local commerce skyrocketed with a great increase in Mississippi River steamboat traffic. The first steamboat to reach the city was called, appropriately enough, the *New Orleans*. By 1840, the city was rated as the world's fourth largest port. By 1850 the population of New Orleans had reached 116,000.

New Orleans is the South's oldest major city.

When Civil War broke out in 1861, the South seemed unaware of how strategic the city's location was. Admiral David Farragut of the Union forces was able to capture it in April 1862. Then it came under the military command of General Benjamin Butler, who earned the city's everlasting hatred for his cruel treatment. A long period of unrest and increasing debt followed the war. By 1900, New Orleans had dropped from third to twelfth place in the national ranking of cities, although its population had increased to more than 287,000.

Today, New Orleans is ranked as the fourth busiest port in the United States. Its population is more than 465,000. It is a favorite of tourists from home and abroad, especially at Mardi Gras, the fabulous carnival celebration before the Christian period of Lent. The modern city of New Orleans retains much of its French and Spanish flavor in its architecture, restaurants, and culture.

Chapter Five
Henry Rowe Schoolcraft:
Where the River Begins (1817–1832)

Henry Rowe Schoolcraft (1793–1864) is rather neglected as an explorer. He is more famous as an ethnologist, one who studies human races. Schoolcraft was a scholar of Native American culture and history. His six volumes entitled *Historical and Statistical Information Respecting the History, Condition, and Prospects of the Indian Tribes of the United States* (1851–1857) contributed greatly to the understanding and study of Native American peoples. His wife was part Ojibway. He became a superintendent of Indian affairs for Michigan, negotiating several treaties between the United States and Native Americans. He was a well-known geologist, one who studies the earth, especially rocks. His *A View of the Lead Mines of Missouri* (1819) won him scientific respect. He was also a glassmaker and wrote a book on that, too.

It would seem that Schoolcraft had little time for other exploring. But in 1832 in northern Minnesota, he came upon a lake. That one discovery put him in the history books under the title of explorer. Schoolcraft had located the source, the beginning, of the mighty Mississippi River.

Father of the waters

Native Americans who lived along the Mississippi had great respect for it. It

A portrait of Henry Rowe Schoolcraft (1793–1864)

was both highway and food source. As European explorers traveled more and more of the river, they, too, began to have respect for it. They also began to realize what a great resource it was and the profitable avenue of trade it offered.

When the Louisiana Territory became part of the United States in 1803, the purchase price was a little more than $27 million. Since the territory was figured to be about 828,000 square miles (2,144,510 square kilometers), that came to three cents an acre. It also made the sale the greatest land bargain in U.S. history.

The problem for President Thomas Jefferson, however, was that no one was exactly sure what he had bought. The wording of the treaty was vague and so were the outlines of the boundaries. Since the Louisiana Purchase was bounded by the outer limits of the Mississippi watershed, all of the land area that drains into the river, it was important that the government know exactly where that river began.

So, the president decided it was time to do more exploring. He sent Meriwether Lewis and William Clark to chart the Louisiana Territory, including the river's major branch, the Missouri. And he sent Zebulon Pike to find the Mississippi's **headwater,** or its source. Pike traveled around Minnesota but never did find where the river began. That would take another 26 years and the explorations of ethnologist Henry Rowe Schoolcraft.

Growing up a scholar

Schoolcraft was born in Albany County, New York, on March 28, 1793. His parents were Margaret Anne Rowe and Lawrence Schoolcraft, a glassmaker. Schoolcraft's great-grandfather, James Calcraft, had emigrated to Albany County from England in 1727. The boy went to public school in Hamilton, New York, and went on to Union College at age fifteen. At Middlebury College, he studied languages, science, and geology, and also took up glassmaking.

For the next few years, Schoolcraft traveled around New York, Vermont, and New Hampshire as a factory manager. In 1817, he wrote a book on glassmaking. Always interested in geology, he traveled west the next year to study minerals in Arkansas and Missouri, a region largely occupied by Native Americans. His report on that expedition was published in New York in 1819. He was already known as a competent geologist, but the report enhanced his scientific reputation. It also gained him a place on an expedition to explore the upper Mississippi and the Lake Superior copper region. The expedition was led by Lewis Cass, governor of the Michigan Territory. Cass had received permission and money from the U.S. secretary of war to try to find the source of the Mississippi River. The expedition apparently came within a three-day journey to the source before the governor gave up. Upon their return, Schoolcraft wrote *Narrative Journal of Travels through the Northwestern Regions of the United States ... to the Mississippi River (1821).*

Native American studies

On his travels, Schoolcraft made friends with many members of Native American cultures in North America. In 1822, with the help of Cass, he was appointed Indian agent in Sault Ste. Marie, Michigan. As an agent for the United

States, he was to carry out negotiations between the government and Native Americans. He also began his lifelong interest in and study of Native American history and culture. After about a year as agent, Schoolcraft married a woman, Jane Johnston, who was herself part Ojibway, had been educated in Europe, and whose grandfather had been a powerful war chief. Schoolcraft's wife was a great help in expanding his knowledge of the customs and legends of these people of the upper midwest.

As Schoolcraft increased his knowledge and understanding of Native Americans, his arrogance over his own expertise increased as well. He was sympathetic to the plight of the Indians but grew **paternalistic** about them. No one knew better than he what was good for them. He was scornful of the ideas of other Indian agents. He despised fur traders from Canada who came into the area. He wanted no interference with what he regarded as his territory and his people. Ironically, at the same time

Schoolcraft travels on the Mississippi River.

that Schoolcraft defended the rights of Native Americans, as an agent he was actively involved in helping the federal government take away their hunting grounds. He did, however, ask the government to teach them agriculture.

For some time, Schoolcraft had been aware that the U.S. government was interested in finding the source of the Mississippi. He knew of the expeditions for that purpose, including that of Pike some 26 years earlier. He also knew that honors would surely fall upon the explorer who found the **headwater.** Luckily, according to Native American stories, the source of the river was somewhere in the vicinity of his own territory. Schoolcraft decided that he himself would discover where the great river began.

Finding the beginning

First, he needed money. In 1832, he requested that the Office of Indian Affairs sponsor an expedition to the Chippewa people, supposedly to settle some trouble among its members. He received a grant of $3,200. In addition, he received a promise of military assistance from Lewis Cass, who had become U.S. secretary of war.

The expedition, which started out in May, was truly impressive. It was as though Schoolcraft wanted to show that the **mission** was really important. In addition to Schoolcraft as the leader, there was also a Fifth U.S. Infantry lieutenant heading the military escort, a surgeon, a reverend from the American Board of Foreign Missions, and a part-Native American interpreter who was also Schoolcraft's brother-in-law. Also included were 20 boatmen.

Even more impressive was the staggering amount of supplies. They included numerous canoes, mounds of beef and pork, sugar, rice, tea, and hundreds of pounds of tobacco for the Native Americans. Added to that were muskets, blankets, axes, fishhooks, mending materials, cooking gear, and countless other necessities. Schoolcraft was determined not to fail for want of a missing item.

By early July, the expedition had reached upper Red Cedar Lake, now Cass Lake, in present-day northern Minnesota. From local people, Schoolcraft learned that a place called Lac La Biche was rumored to be the start of the Mississippi. However, the area was swampy and only a few of his canoes could make the journey.

Schoolcraft, the lieutenant, the surgeon, the minister, the interpreter, and an Native American guide named Yellow Head, along with Native Americans to paddle the canoes, began the search for Lac La Biche on July 10. They traveled for three days. When they came to the head of a small stream, Yellow Head told them to **debark.** They followed the guide until they broke out of a clearing. There it was—the small Y-shaped lake that Schoolcraft called Itasca, where the Mississippi begins. The name comes from the Latin *veritas caput*, which is translated as "true head." Schoolcraft

Lake Itasca is now known to be the source of the Mississippi River.

put the two Latin words together and linked the syllables: ver ITAS CAput.

Schoolcraft and his small party sailed around the lake. Since they saw no other outlet, they believed they had found the true source. They raised an American flag and fired a salute from their muskets. The ceremony over, Schoolcraft went home. In 1834, he published *Narrative of an Expedition through the Upper Mississippi to Itasca Lake, the Actual Source of the Mississippi.*

Back to ethnology

For the rest of his life, Schoolcraft went back to being an ethnologist. Always interested in fostering the study of Native Americans, he helped to found the Historical Society of Michigan in 1828. Because the U.S. government wanted more information about Native Americans, his work was encouraged. In 1836, he was promoted to the position of superintendent of Indian affairs for Michigan.

Schoolcraft supported government-sponsored as well as **mission** schools, believing that it was necessary for Native Americans to become Christians before they were educated. His treaty of March 28, 1836, with the Ojibway put much of northern Michigan into U.S. hands. But it did provide for compensation to be paid to individual Native Americans rather than to their tribal chiefs in a lump sum.

Henry Rowe Schoolcraft died in Washington, D.C., on December 10, 1864. His first wife had died in 1842. He was survived by his second wife, Mary Howard of Beaufort District, North Carolina, whom he had married in 1847.

Schoolcraft's real legacy was his many publications describing Native American life and culture. The most famous are his six volumes published between 1851 and 1857. Others include *Algic Researches* (2 volumes, 1839), *Oneota*, which detailed mental abilities (1944–1945), *Notes on the*

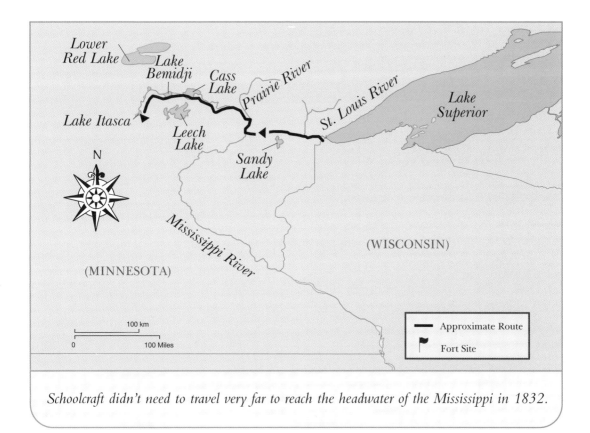

Schoolcraft didn't need to travel very far to reach the headwater of the Mississippi in 1832.

Iroquois (1847), *and Personal Memories … of Thirty Years with the Indian Tribes* (1851). These accounts were more literary than scientific, which was the style of the time. But they proved to be important contributions to the study of early Native Americans.

The explorer part of Henry Schoolcraft was extraordinarily proud of "finding" the source of the Mississippi River. He would have disdained the few instances of people claiming he was wrong. In 1836, for example, four years after Schoolcraft's expedition, Frenchmen Joseph Nicollet did a little exploring of his own in northern Minnesota. His maps of Lake Itasca showed other smaller streams entering into it. Later, in the 1880s, a Captain Willard Glazier published a book claiming he had found the true source upstream from Itasca. He was later discredited by historian and anthropologist Jacob V. Brower, who went to the area in the late 1880s to settle the matter.

Some sources do list other lakes, but most identify Itasca as the true source of the Mississippi. For that, Henry Rowe Schoolcraft, part-time explorer, stays in the history books.

Epilogue:

What Did They Find?

The early native peoples of North America grew up hearing about the mighty river. Many of them lived on its banks. They had no idea it was the great waterway of the continent. They did not know where it began or where it ended. But when explorers came down from Canada or around the Gulf of Mexico in the 1600s and 1700s, they were told of the Missi Sipi, Father of the Waters. And as explorers usually do, they set out to find what they had not seen before.

The six explorers in this book were seeking the Mississippi for many reasons. There was personal fame, and possibly fortune, and the glory of the homeland, of course.

There was curiosity, too. Explorers are naturally curious people. There was the great thrill of adventure. Most explorers are naturally adventurous people, too. As each of the six learned a little more about the river and its valley, they added to the growing knowledge about the vast and new—for them—territory that was North America. Exploration is a growing thing. Each explorer learns from those who have gone before.

From 1673, when Marquette and Jolliet reached the Mississippi, until 1832, when Schoolcraft found its source, knowledge about the river was growing. When Marquette and Jolliet first saw it, they had no idea of its size or where it flowed. When Schoolcraft looked on Lake Itasca, the young United States was just beginning to understand how important this river really was. It would become a key factor in the development of North America, a major waterway for trade and transportation. That is still true today.

These explorers from Canada and Europe were not the first to see the Mississippi River or its valley. They were not even the first to understand fully its importance. But they were the first to chart its waters, the first to learn how far it went, and the first to learn where it flowed. That is why they are important.

Important Events in the Exploration of the Mississippi River Valley

1672 Marquette meets Jolliet at Michilimackinac trading post, December 8

1673 The explorers set out to find the Mississippi, May 17; reach the river, June 17, at **Prairie** du Chien, WI

1679 La Salle builds *Griffon,* first commercial vessel to enter Lake Erie

1680 La Salle builds fort on Lake Peoria, first sees the Mississippi

1681 La Salle expedition leaves for the Mississippi, December 21

1682 La Salle expedition enters the river, February 6; reaches **delta,** April 6; La Salle claims Louisiana territory for France, April 9

1683 La Salle builds Fort St. Louis on Illinois River

1684 La Salle leads expedition to build colony at mouth of the river, July 24; unable to find mouth from the Gulf of Mexico

1698 Iberville sent by France to found colony at mouth of river, October 2

1699 Iberville reaches Gulf of Mexico; finds delta and explores upriver in March; was first European to see Lake Pontchartrain; established Fort Maurepas, or Old Biloxi

1700? Iberville builds Fort La Boulaye south of present-day New Orleans; Bienville explores Red River

1702 Bienville in charge; colony moved to present-day Mobile, Alabama

1716 Bienville wages war against Natchez

1717 Bienville lays out plan for New Orleans

1722 New Orleans becomes capital of the territory

1763 Louisiana Territory ceded to Spain

1800 France reclaims Louisiana

1803 Louisiana Territory sold to the United States

1804 Meriwether Lewis and William Clark begin their exploration of the Missouri River, part of the Mississippi River system

1832 Schoolcraft finds source of the Mississippi at Lake Itasca, Minnesota

Important Sites Along the Mississippi River System

The Mississippi River system is largely responsible for the settling and growth of these major U.S. cities:

Cincinnati, Ohio

Founded: 1788 as Losantiville

Named for: Revolutionary War Officers' Society of the Cincinnati (1790), which took its name from Roman soldier Lucius Quinctius Cincinnatus

Location: Between Little Miami and Great Miami rivers were they flow into the Ohio River

Population: 336,400

Noted for: manufacturing, inland port

Kansas City, Missouri

Founded: French fur traders, 1821; named Town of Kansas, 1850; present name, 1889

Named for: Kansas River

Location: Missouri River at mouth of Kansas River

Population: 441,574; metro area 1,979,202

Noted for: major agricultural market, livestock exchange

Louisville, Kentucky

Founded: 1779 by settlers with George Rogers Clark

Named for: Louis XVI of France

Location: Ohio River, southern shore

Population: 255,045; metro area 1,025,598

Noted for: state's largest city; manufacturing center; horseracing

Memphis, Tennessee

Founded: 1819 on site of Chickasaw village and U.S. fort (1797)

Named for: Ancient Egyptian city on the Nile River

Location: Mississippi River at meeting of Arkansas, Mississippi, and Tennessee borders

Population: 603,507; metro area 1,135,618

Noted for: major inland river port and railroad terminal; largest hardwood lumber center; major cotton market

Minneapolis, Minnesota

Founded: 1844 as village of St. Anthony by missionary Louis Hennepin; Incorporated with present name 1856

Named for: Dakota Sioux word *minne*, meaning "water," and Greek *polis*, meaning "city"

Location: Mississippi River, opposite St. Paul, near mouth of Minnesota River

Population: 351,731; metro area 2,968,806

Noted for: commercial/industrial center of large agricultural area

New Orleans, Louisiana

Founded: 1718 by Jean-Baptiste Le Moyne de Bienville for France

Named for: Philippe II, duc d'Orleans

60

Location: Mississippi River, 110 miles upriver from the Gulf of Mexico

Population: 465,000; metro area 1,337,726

Noted for: nation's fourth largest port; tourism

Omaha, Nebraska

Founded: 1854 after visits by Lewis and Clark (1804) and fur trader Manuel Lisa

Named for: Omaha Indians; name means "upstream people"

Location: Missouri River west bank, opposite Council Bluffs, IA

Population: 371,291; metro area 712,738

Noted for: agriculture market, meat-packing, livestock center

Pittsburgh, Pennsylvania

Founded: 1764 by John Campbell in area around Fort Pitt

Named for: English statesman Willliam Pitt the elder

Location: Confluence of Allegheny and Monongahela Rivers, which unite to form the Ohio River

Population: 371,291; metro area 2,358,695

Noted for: large inland port and transportation center; industrial research lab center; coal, coke, and chemical products

Saint Louis, Missouri

Founded: 1764 by fur trader Pierre Laclede Liguest of New Orleans

Named for: Louis XV of France

Location: Mississippi River, 10 miles (16 kilometers) below meeting with the Missouri

Population: 339,316; metro area 2,603,607

Noted for: state's largest city; major transportation hub; livestock, grain, lumber market; manufacturing center

Mississippi River System Fact List

Name of River	Location	Source/Mouth	Length (mi)
Mississippi	central U.S.	Lake Itasca, MN/ Gulf of Mexico	2,350
Missouri	central-western U.S.	Jefferson, Madison, Gallatin Rivers, MT/ joins Mississippi	2,315
Ohio	eastern-central U.S.	Allegheny, Monangahela Rivers, PA / joins Mississippi	981

Drainage basin: approx. 1,200,000 square miles (3,107,985 square kilometers); all/part of 31 states and two Canadian provinces

Glossary

administration process of performing executive duties

alliance connection between people, parties, or states for common interest of all

channel bed where a natural stream of water runs

confederacy body formed by persons, states, or nations; e.g., when the southern states seceded from the United States in 1861, they formed the Confederate States of America.

debark leave a ship

delta soil deposit at mouth of a river, named for the fourth letter of the Greek alphabet (symbol for a capital delta is a triangle)

epidemic outbreak or sudden rapid growth of disease within a population

exploit deed or heroic act; as a verb, to take advantage of

gesture use of limbs or body to express something

headwater source, or beginning, of a stream of water, usually expressed in plural

mediator one who intervenes between opposing parties

mission an organization to carry on religious or humanitarian work

monopoly sole possession or control

outpost frontier settlement

paternalistic attitude of person in authority to supply needs or regulate conduct in matters affecting people as individuals

portage to carry boats or canoes overland from one body of water to another

prairie large area of level or rolling land, common in Mississippi Valley

rapids part of a river where the current is fast and surface usually broken by rocks or other obstructions

sieur French word meaning "sir" or "master," as in Sieur de Bienville

Further Reading

Baker, Daniel. *World Explorers and Discoverers*. Farmington Hills, Mich.: Gale Group, 1993.

Harmon, Daniel E. *Jolliet and Marquette: Explorers of the Mississippi River*. Broomall, Pa.: Chelsea House, 2001.

Jacobs, William Jay. *La Salle: A Life of Boundless Adventure*. New York: Watts, 1994.

Saari, Peggy, and Daniel B. Baker. *Explorers & Discoverers*. Detroit: Gale, 1998.

Waldman, Carl, and Alan Wexler. *Who Was Who in World Exploration*. Bridgewater, N.J.: Replica, 1999.

Index

Beaujeu, Tanguy de 29, 30

Belle 31, 33

Bienville, Jean-Baptiste (see Le Moyne, Jean-Baptiste, Sieur de Bienville)

blacks 47–48

Bonaparte, Napoleon 50

Brower, Jacob V. 57

Buade, Louis de, Comte de Frontenac 13, 22, 23, 28, 32

Cadillac, Antoine Laumet (see La Mothe, Antoine Laumet de, Sieur de Cadillac)

Cass, Lewis 53, 54, 55

Cavelier, Rene-Robert (see La Salle, Rene-Robert Cavelier, Sieur de La Salle)

Clark, William 53

colonization 5, 6, 8, 9, 13, 18, 19, 20, 29, 30, 32, 34, 35, 38, 39, 40–41, 43, 44, 45, 46, 49, 50

Company of the Indies 46, 48

England 13, 22, 34, 35, 36, 37, 38, 40, 41, 42, 43, 47, 50

explorers 7, 8, 11, 13, 16, 41, 52, 58

Fort Heartbreak 25, 26, 27

France 13, 19, 22, 29, 34, 35, 37, 40, 41, 43, 47, 50

French and Indian War 50

Frontenac, Louis de Buade (see Buade, Louis de, Comte de Frontenac)

fur trade 10, 12, 18, 20, 22, 23, 35, 46

Glazier, Willard 57

Griffon 23–25, 26

Gulf of Mexico 8, 16, 19, 27, 28, 29, 33, 38, 40, 41, 43, 50, 58

Hennepin, Louis 22, 25

Iberville, Pierre (see Le Moyne, Pierre, Sieur d'Iberville)

Iroquois Confederation 13, 20

Itasca, Lake 55, 56, 57, 58

Jefferson, Thomas 53

Jolliet, Louis 5, 6, 7, 8, 12–17, 18, 22, 58

Joutel, Henri 31, 32

La Salle, Rene-Robert Cavelier, Sieur de 5, 6, 19–32, 37, 38

Lac La Biche 55

Le Mothe, Antoine Laumet de, Sieur de Cadillac 45, 46

Le Moyne, Jean-Baptiste, Sieur de Bienville 5, 6, 7, 36, 38, 41, 42, 50

Le Moyne, Pierre, Sieur d'Iberville 5, 6, 7, 34–41, 42, 43, 44

Le Moyne, Sauvole 38, 39, 40, 43, 44

Lefebre, Joseph Antoine, Sieur de la Barre 29

Lewis, Meriwether 53

Louis XIV (king of France) 9, 19, 20, 22, 23, 28, 29, 30, 35, 37, 39, 41

Louisiana 6, 19, 34, 37, 39, 40, 41, 42, 44, 45, 46, 47, 48, 49, 50

Louisiana Purchase 53

Louisiana Territory 52–53

Marquette, Jacques 5, 6, 7, 8–12, 13–18, 22, 58

Mississippi River 5, 8, 13, 15, 20–21, 22, 25, 27, 31, 50, 53, 58

course 8

delta 28, 29, 38, 43

importance 5, 8, 52, 58

mouth 8, 16, 19, 22, 27, 29, 30, 31, 34, 38, 39, 43, 50

names 8, 15, 20

size 5, 8

source 8, 52, 53, 55–56, 57, 58

system 5, 8, 16

tributaries 5, 8

Mississippi River Valley 5, 28, 40

Missouri River 5, 8, 25, 53

Moranget, Crevel de 32

natives 7, 8, 9, 10–11, 12–13, 14–15, 20, 24, 27–28, 29, 32, 41, 43, 44, 48, 52, 53, 54, 55, 56, 58

Bayagoula 38–39, 43

Chickasaw 48, 49

Huron 10, 11

Illinois 10, 11, 17

Iroquois 10, 12, 21, 22, 27

Masacouten 15

Natchez 46, 48, 49

Ojibway 8, 10, 56

Ottawa 10, 11

Peoria 15

Quapaw 15–16

Seneca 20

Sioux 11, 25

New France 9, 12, 20, 22, 23, 34

New Orleans 5, 6, 42, 47, 48, 50–51

New World 4, 9, 22

Nicollet, Joseph 57

Northwest Passage 21, 35

Ohio River 5, 8, 15, 19, 20, 22

Schoolcraft, Henry Rowe 5, 6, 7, 52, 53–57, 58

Spain 16, 29, 40, 41, 42, 47, 49, 50

Tonti, Henri de 23, 24, 25, 26, 27, 29, 32, 38, 43

United States 5, 6, 50, 52, 58

Yellow Head 55